- *Ten Commandments* -

THE LAW OF GOD

DR. JAEROCK LEE

If you love Me, you will keep My commandments.

(John 14:15)

THE LAW OF GOD by Dr. Jaerock Lee
Published by Urim Books (Representative: Kyungtae Noh)
73, Yeouidaebang-ro 22-gil, Dongjak-Gu, Seoul, Korea
www.urimbooks.com

All rights reserved. This book or parts thereof may not be reproduced in any form, stored in a retrieval system, or transmitted in any form or by any means, electronic, mechanical, photocopying, recording or otherwise, without prior written permission of the publisher.

Unless otherwise noted, all Scripture quotations are taken from the Holy Bible, NEW AMERICAN STANDARD BIBLE, ®, Copyright © 1960, 1962, 1963, 1968, 1971, 1972, 1973, 1975, 1977, 1995 by The Lockman Foundation. Used by permission.

Copyright © 2009 by Dr. Jaerock Lee
ISBN: 978-89-7557-292-0, ISBN: 978-89-7557-060-5(set)
Translated by Dr. Esther K. Chung. Used by permission.

Previously published in Korean by Urim Books, Seoul, Korea.
Copyright © 2007, ISBN: 978-89-7557-098-8, ISBN: 978-89-7557-067-4(set)

First Published November 2009

Edited by Dr. Geumsun Vin
Designed by Editorial Bureau of Urim Books
Printed by Yewon Printing Company
For more information contact; urimbook@hotmail.com

Preface

While ministering, I receive numerous questions such as, "Where is God?" or "Show me God," or "How can I meet God?" People ask these kinds of questions because they don't know how to meet God. But the way to meeting God is much easier than we think. We can meet God simply by learning His commandments and obeying them. However, although many people know this fact with their heads, they fail to obey the commandments because they don't understand the actual spiritual significance captured in each commandment, which came out as a result of the Father's deep love for us.

Just as one individual needs proper education to prepare to face society, a child of God also needs proper education to be prepared to face heaven. This is where the laws of God come in. The laws of God, or His Ten Commandments, should be taught to every new child of God, and applied in every Christian's life.

"The Law of God" is commandments that God created for us as a way of getting closer to Him, getting answers from Him, and being together with Him. In other words, learning the *"The Law of God"* is our ticket to meeting God.

Around 1446 B.C., just after the Israelites left Egypt, God wanted to lead them into the land flowing with milk and honey, otherwise known as the land of Canaan. In order for this to happen, the Israelites needed to understand God's will, and they also needed to know what it truly means to become children of God. That is why God lovingly inscribed the Ten Commandments, which concisely sums up all of His laws, onto two stone tablets (Exodus 24:12). He then gave these tablets to Moses so he could educate the Israelites on how to get where God wants them to be, which is precisely, in His presence, by teaching them the duties as children of God.

About thirty years ago, after I met the living God, I came to learn and obey His laws while attending church and seeking out every revival I could find. Beginning with giving up smoking and drinking, I came to learn about keeping the Sabbath day holy, giving faithful tithes, praying, etc. In a little notebook, I began jotting down the sins that I couldn't cast off right away. Then I prayed and fasted, asking God to help me obey His commands. The blessing I received as a result was amazing!

First, God blessed our family physically so none of us ever got sick. Then He gave us so much financial blessings that we could freely focus on helping those in need. Lastly, He poured so much spiritual blessings upon me that I am now able to lead a global ministry aimed at world evangelism and missions.

If you learn God's commandments and obey them, not only will you be prosperous in all areas of your life, but you will also be able to experience glory as bright as the sun, once you enter into His eternal kingdom.

This book *The Law of God* is a compilation of the series of sermons based on His word, and the inspiration about "The Ten Commandments" which I received while fasting and praying shortly after I began my ministry. Through these messages, many believers came to understand God's love, began living a life of obedience to His commandments, and thereby prospered spiritually and in all other areas of their lives. Furthermore, many believers experienced receiving the answer to their every prayer. Most importantly, they all came to have a greater hope for heaven.

So if you come to know the spiritual significance of the Ten Commandments that are discussed in this book, and come to understand the deep love of God who gave us the Ten Commandments and decide to live in obedience to His commandments, I can guarantee that you will receive incredible blessings from the Lord. In Deuteronomy 28:1-2, it says that you will be blessed at all times. *"Now it shall be, if you diligently obey the LORD your God, being careful to do all His commandments which I command you today, the LORD your God will set you high above all the nations of the earth. All these blessings will come upon you and overtake you if you obey the LORD your God."*

I'd like to thank Geumsun Vin, the Director of the Editorial Bureau, Urim Books, and her staff for their unmatched dedication and priceless contribution to the making of this book. I also pray in the name of our Lord that all those who come across this book will easily come to understand the laws of God, and obey His commandments to become a more loved, and therefore more blessed child of God!

Jaerock Lee

Introduction

We give all glory to God the Father for allowing us to collect the study of the Ten Commandments, which contains God's heart and will, into this book, *The Law of God*.

First, "God's Love Captured in the Ten Commandments," fills the reader with the necessary background information about the Ten Commandments. It answers the question, "What exactly are the Ten Commandments?" This chapter also explains that God gave us the Ten Commandments because He loves us, and He ultimately wants to bless us. So when we obey each commandment with the power of God's love, then we can receive all the blessings He has in store for us.

In "The First Commandment," we learn that if anyone loves God, he or she can easily obey His commandments. This chapter also goes over the question of why as the first commandment God commands us not to put any other gods before Him.

"The Second Commandment" covers the importance of never worshipping false idols—or in a spiritual sense—having anything that one may love more than God. Here, we also learn about the spiritual consequences of when we worship false idols and when we don't, and the specific blessings and curses that come into our lives as a result.

The chapter on "The Third Commandment" explains what it means to take the LORD's name in vain, and what one should do to avoid committing this.

In "The Fourth Commandment" we learn about the true meaning of the "Sabbath," and why the Sabbath changed from Saturday to Sunday, moving from the Old Testament to the New Testament. This chapter also explains exactly how one should keep the Sabbath day holy, mainly in three different ways. This chapter also depicts the conditions for which exceptions to this commandment may apply—when working and business transactions on the Sabbath day can be permitted.

"The Fifth Commandment" explains in detail how one should honor their parents in a godly way. We also learn about what it means to honor God, who is the Father of our spirits, and what types of blessings we receive when we honor Him, and our physical parents, in His truth.

The chapter on "The Sixth Commandment" consists of two parts: the first part focuses on the sin of committing physical murder, and the second part is a spiritual explanation of committing the sin of murder inside one's heart, which many believers may be guilty of committing, but seldom realize they are committing.

"The Seventh Commandment" goes over the sin of physically committing adultery and the sin of committing adultery in one's heart or mind, which is actually the scarier of the two sins. This chapter also goes over the spiritual significance of committing this sin, and the process of prayer and fasting, by which one can throw away this sin through the help of the Holy Spirit and God's grace and power.

"The Eighth Commandment" describes the physical definition of stealing, and the spiritual definition of stealing. This chapter also specifically explains how one may commit the sin of stealing from God by failing to give his tithes and offerings, or even by mishandling God's word.

"The Ninth Commandment" deals with the three different types of giving false testimony, or lying. This chapter also emphasizes how one can pull out the root of deceit from his heart by filling his heart with the truth instead.

"The Tenth Commandment" explains about the instances where we can sin as a result of coveting our neighbor. We also learn here that true blessing is when our soul prospers, because when our soul prospers, we receive the blessing of being prosperous in all areas of our life.

Finally, in the last chapter, "The Law of Abiding with God," as we study the ministry of Jesus Christ who fulfilled the Law with love, we learn that we must have love in order to fulfill God's word. We also learn about the kind of love that even extends beyond justice.

I hope that this text will help you, the reader, clearly understand the spiritual significance of the Ten Commandments. And as you obey the LORD's commandments, may you always be in the bright presence of God. I also pray in the name of our Lord that while fulfilling His laws, you come to the place in your spiritual life where all your prayers are answered, and His blessings overflow upon all areas of your life!

Geumsun Vin
Director of the Editorial Bureau

Table of Contents

Preface
Introduction

Chapter 1
God's Love Captured
in the Ten Commandments … 1

Chapter 2 : The First Commandment
"You Shall Have No Other Gods before Me" … 13

Chapter 3 : The Second Commandment
"You Shall Not Make for Yourself
an Idol or Worship It" … 29

Chapter 4 : The Third Commandment
"You Shall Not Take the Name of the LORD
Your God in Vain" … 49

Chapter 5 : The Fourth Commandment
"Remember the Sabbath Day, to Keep It Holy" … 65

Chapter 6 : The Fifth Commandment
"Honor Your Father and Your Mother"   83

Chapter 7 : The Sixth Commandment
"You Shall Not Murder"   97

Chapter 8 : The Seventh Commandment
"You Shall Not Commit Adultery"   113

Chapter 9 : The Eighth Commandment
"You Shall Not Steal"   129

Chapter 10 : The Ninth Commandment
"You Shall Not Bear False Witness
against Your Neighbor"   145

Chapter 11 : The Tenth Commandment
"You Shall Not Covet Your Neighbor's House"   159

Chapter 12
The Law of Abiding with God   173

Chapter 1

God's Love Captured in the Ten Commandments

Exodus 20:5-6

You shall not worship them or serve them; for I, the LORD your God, am a jealous God, visiting the iniquity of the fathers on the children, on the third and the fourth generations of those who hate Me, but showing lovingkindness to thousands, to those who love Me and keep My commandments.

Four thousand years ago, God chose Abraham as the father of faith. God blessed Abraham and made a covenant with him, promising him descendents "as numerous as the stars in the sky and as the sand on the seashore."

And in His time, God faithfully formed the nation of Israel through the twelve sons of Abraham's grandson, Jacob. Under God's provision, Jacob and his sons moved to Egypt to avoid a famine and lived there for 400 years. This was all part of God's loving plan to protect them from the invasion of Gentile nations until they could grow into a larger and stronger nation.

Jacob's family grew from what consisted of seventy people— when they first moved into Egypt—into a number great enough to form one nation. And as this nation grew stronger, God chose one individual by the name of Moses to become the leader of the Israelites. Then God led these people to the Promised Land of Canaan, the land flowing with milk and honey.

The Ten Commandments were the loving words that God gave to the Israelites while leading them to this Promised Land.

In order for the Israelites to enter into the blessed land of Canaan, they had to meet two qualifications: they had to have faith in God; and they had to obey Him. However, without a set standard for their faith and obedience, they wouldn't have understood what it truly means to have faith and to be obedient. This is why God gave them the Ten Commandments through their leader Moses.

The Ten Commandments are a list of rules that set a standard for human beings to follow, but God did not autocratically force them to obey these commandments. Only after showing them and making them experience His miraculous power—by sending the ten plagues on Egypt, dividing the Red Sea, changing the bitter water into sweet water at Marah, feeding the Israelites with manna and quail—did He give them the Ten Commandments to follow.

The most important piece of information here is that every word of God, including the Ten Commandments, wasn't just given to the Israelites, but to all those who believe in Him today, as a shortcut to receiving His love and blessings.

The Heart of God Who Gave the Commandments

When childrearing, parents teach countless rules to their children; rules such as "You must wash your hands after playing outside," or "Always cover yourself with a blanket while sleeping," or "Never cross the street when the pedestrian signal is red."

Parents don't bombard their children with all these rules

to give them a hard time. They teach all these rules to their children because they love them. It's naturally parents' desire to want to protect their children from diseases and dangers, to keep them safe, and to help them live peacefully throughout their entire lives. This is the same reason God gave the Ten Commandments to us, His children: because He loves us.

In Exodus 15:26, God says, *"If you will give earnest heed to the voice of the LORD your God, and do what is right in His sight, and give ear to His commandments, and keep all His statutes, I will put none of the diseases on you which I have put on the Egyptians; for I, the LORD, am your healer."*
In Leviticus 26:3-5, He says, *"If you walk in My statutes and keep My commandments so as to carry them out, then I shall give you rains in their season, so that the land will yield its produce and the trees of the field will bear their fruit. Indeed, your threshing will last for you until grape gathering, and grape gathering will last until sowing time. You will thus eat your food to the full and live securely in your land."*

God gave us the commandments so we can know how to meet Him, receive His blessings and the answers to our prayers, and ultimately live with peace and joy in our lives.

Another reason why we need to obey God's laws, including the Ten Commandments, is because of the just laws of the spiritual world. Just as every nation has its own laws, God's kingdom has spiritual laws that were set up by God. Although God created the universe and He is the Creator who has absolute control over life, death, curses, and blessings, He is not a totalitarian. This is why even though He is the Creator of the laws, He Himself strictly abides by these laws.

Just as we abide by the laws of the country we're citizens of, if we have accepted Jesus Christ as our Savior and have become children of God and thus citizens of His kingdom, then we should rightfully abide by the laws of God and His kingdom.

In 1 Kings 2:3 it is written, *"Keep the charge of the LORD your God, to walk in His ways, to keep His statutes, His commandments, His ordinances, and His testimonies, according to what is written in the Law of Moses, that you may succeed in all that you do and wherever you turn."*

Abiding by God's laws means obeying the words of God, including the Ten Commandments, which are recorded in the Bible. When you abide by these laws, you can receive God's protection and blessings and prosper wherever you go.

On the contrary, when you break God's laws, the enemy Satan has the right to bring temptations and hardships to you, so God cannot protect you. To break God's commands is to sin, and thus it is to become a slave to sin and Satan, who will ultimately lead you to hell.

God Wants to Bless Us

So the main reason God gave us the Ten Commandments is because He loves us and wants to bless us. Not only does He want us to experience eternal blessings in heaven, but He also wants us to receive His blessings on earth and be prosperous in whatever we do here as well. When we realize this love of God, we can only be thankful to God for giving us the commandments and happily obey His commands.

We can see that children, once they truly realize how much their parents love them, try hard to obey their parents. Even if they fail to obey their parents and are disciplined, because they understand that their parents are acting out of love, they might say, "Mommy/Daddy, I'll try to be better next time," and lovingly run into their parents' arms. And as they mature and have a deeper understanding of their parents' love and concern for them, children will abide by their parents' teachings to bring them joy.

Their parents' true love is what gives these children the power to obey. This is the same as us abiding by all of God's words that are recorded in the Bible. People try their best to abide by the commandments once they come to understand that God loved us so much that He sent His one and only Son, Jesus Christ, into this world to die on the cross for us.

In fact, the greater the faith we have in the fact that this

Jesus Christ, who had no sin whatsoever, took all kinds of persecution as He died on the cross for our sins, the greater the joy we have as we obey these commandments.

The Blessings We Receive When We Abide by His Commandments

Our forefathers of faith, who obeyed God's every word and lived strictly according to His commandments, received great blessings and glorified God the Father with all their hearts. And today, they are shining on us the eternal light of truth that never burns out.

Abraham, Daniel, and the apostle Paul are some of these people of faith. And even today, there are people of faith who continue to do as these people did.

For example, the sixteenth president of the United States, Abraham Lincoln only had nine months of schooling, but because of his praiseworthy character and virtues, he is loved and respected by many people today. Abraham's mother, Nancy Hanks Lincoln, passed away when Lincoln was only nine, but while she was alive, she taught him to memorize short verses from the Bible and obey God's commandments.

And when she knew she was going to die, she called her son and left him these last words, "I want you to love God and obey His commandments." As Abraham Lincoln matured, became a famous politician, and changed history with his movement to abolish slavery, the sixty-six books of the Bible were always by his side. For people like Lincoln, who stay close to God and abide by His words, God always shows them the evidence of His love.

It was not long after I first started our church that I made a visit to a couple that was married for many years but couldn't bear children. With guidance of the Holy Spirit, I led worship and blessed the couple. Then I made a request. I asked that they keep the Sabbath day holy by worshipping God every Sunday, make tithes, and obey the Ten Commandments.

This newly believing couple began to attend worship every Sunday and give tithes, according to God's commands. As a result, they received the blessing of childbirth and gave birth to healthy children. Not only that, they received great financial blessings as well. Now, the husband serves the church as an elder, and the whole family is a big supporter in relief and evangelism.

Abiding by God's commands is like holding a lamp in complete darkness. When we have a bright lamp, we don't have to worry about tripping over something in the dark. Likewise, when God, who is light, is with us, He protects us in all circumstances, and we are able to enjoy the blessings and authority that's reserved for all children of God.

The Key to Receiving Everything that You Ask for

In 1 John 3:21-22 it says, *"If our heart does not condemn us, we have confidence before God; and whatever we ask we receive from Him, because we keep His commandments and do the things that are pleasing in His sight."*

Isn't it great to know that if we just obey the commands written in the Bible and do what pleases God, we can boldly ask anything of Him and He will answer us? How happy God must be, watching over His obedient children with His fiery eyes and being able to answer their every prayer, according to the laws of the spiritual world!

This is why God's Ten Commandments is like a textbook of love that teaches us the best way to receive God's blessings while being cultivated on this earth. The Commandments teach us how we can avoid calamities or disasters and how we can receive blessings.

God didn't give us the commandments to punish those who don't obey them, but to let us enjoy the eternal blessings in His beautiful kingdom of heaven by obeying His commandments (1 Timothy 2:4). When you come to feel and understand God's heart and live by His commandments, you can receive even more of His love.

Furthermore, as you study each commandment more

closely, and as you completely obey each commandment with the strength that God lovingly provides you, you should be able to receive all the blessings you want to receive from Him.

Chapter 2
The First Commandment

"You Shall Have No Other Gods before Me"

Exodus 20:1-3

Then God spoke all these words, saying,

"I am the LORD your God, who brought you out of the land of Egypt, out of the house of slavery. You shall have no other gods before Me."

Two people who love each other feel joy just by being together. That's why two lovers don't even feel the cold when spending time together in the middle of winter, and that's why they can do whatever the other asks them to do, no matter how hard the task, as long as it makes the other person happy. Even if they have to sacrifice themselves for the other person, they feel happy that they can do something for the other person, and they feel happy when they see the joy on the other person's face.

This is similar to our love for God. If we truly love God, then obeying His commandments should not be burdensome; rather, it should bring us joy.

The Ten Commandments that God's Children Should Obey

Today, some people who call themselves believers say, "How can we obey *all* of God's Ten Commandments?" They're basically saying because people aren't perfect, there's no way we can completely obey the Ten Commandments. We can only try to obey all the Commandments.

But in 1 John 5:3, it is written, *"For this is the love of God, that we keep His commandments; and His commandments are not burdensome."* This means that the proof that we love God is our obedience to His commands, and His commands are not burdensome enough that we cannot obey them.

In the Old Testament times, people had to obey the commandments with their own will and strength, but now in the New Testament times, anyone who accepts Jesus Christ as his Savior receives the Holy Spirit who helps him obey.

The Holy Spirit is one with God, and as God's heart, the Holy Spirit has the role of helping God's children. That's why the Holy Spirit at times intercedes for us, comforts us, guides our actions, and pours out the love of God upon us so that we can fight against sin, even to the point of shedding blood, and act according to God's will (Acts 9:31, 20:28; Romans 5:5, 8:26).

When we receive this strength from the Holy Spirit, we can deeply understand the love of God that gave us His one and only Son, and then we can easily obey what we can't obey with our own will and strength. There are people who still say it's difficult to obey God's commands and don't even try to obey them. And they continue to live in the midst of sin. These people don't really love God from the depths of their hearts.

In 1 John 1:6 it says, *"If we say that we have fellowship with Him and yet walk in the darkness, we lie and do not practice the truth"* and in 1 John 2:4, it says, *"The one who says, 'I have come to know Him,' and does not keep His commandments, is a liar, and the truth is not in him."*

If God's word, which is the truth and the seed of life, is in someone, he cannot sin. He will be led to live in the truth. So if someone claims to believe in God but does not obey His commandments, that means the truth is not really in him, and he is lying before God.

Then what is the very first of these commandments that God's children need to obey, that proves their love for Him?

"You Shall Have No Other Gods before Me"

The "You" here is referring to Moses, who directly received the Ten Commandments from God, the Israelites who received the commandments through Moses, and all of God's children today that are saved by the name of the Lord. Why do you think God commands His people not to put other gods before Him as the very first commandment?

This is because God alone is the true, one and only living God, the omnipotent Creator of the universe. Also, only God has supreme control over the universe, the history of mankind, life and death, and He gives true life and eternal life to man.

God is the One who saved us from our bondage of sin in this world. This is why aside from the one and only God, we must not put any other gods in our hearts.

But many foolish people distance themselves from God and spend their lives worshipping many false idols. Some worship the image of Buddha, who can't even blink, some worship stones, some worship old trees, and some even face the North Pole and worship it.

Some people worship nature and they call out to the names of the so many false gods by idolizing dead people. Every race and every nation has its own share of idols. Just in Japan alone they have so many idols that they say they have eight million different gods.

So why do you think people make all these false idols and worship them? This is because they're looking for a way to comfort themselves, or they're just following their ancestors' old customs that just happen to be wrong. Or, they may also have a selfish desire to receive more blessings or more good fortunes by worshipping many different gods.

But one thing we must make clear is that aside from God the Creator, no other god has the power to give us blessings, let alone to save us.

Evidences in Nature of God the Creator

It is written in Romans 1:20, *"For since the creation of the world His invisible attributes, His eternal power and divine nature, have been clearly seen, being understood through what has been made, so that they are without excuse."* If we look at the principles of the universe, we can see that an absolute Creator exists, and that there is only one God the Creator.

For example, when we look at the human race on this earth, all people's bodies have the same structure and function. Whether a person is black or white, no matter what race they are, or what country they're from, they have two eyes, two ears, one nose, and one mouth, located at about the same place of the face. Furthermore, this is the same case with animals as well.

Elephants are animals with long noses. But notice how they have one long nose, and two nostrils. Rabbits, with long ears, and fierce lions also have the same number of eyes, mouth, and ears located in the same area as people. Countless living organisms, like animals, fish, birds, and even insects—aside from the special characteristics that make them different from one another—have the same bodily structure and function. This proves that there is one creator.

Natural phenomena also clearly prove the existence of God the Creator. Once a day, the earth makes one complete rotation on its axis, and once a year, it makes one complete revolution around the sun, and once a month, the moon rotates and revolves around the earth. Due to these rotations and revolutions, we can experience many natural occurrences on a regular basis. We have night and day, and the four different seasons. We have high tide and low tide, and due to thermal changes we experience atmospheric circulation.

The location and movement of the earth makes this planet a perfect habitat for the survival of mankind, and all other living organisms. The distance between the sun and the earth couldn't have been closer, or further away. The distance between the sun and the earth has always been at the most perfect distance since the beginning of time, and the earth's rotation and revolution around the sun have been occurring for a very long time, without a fraction of an error.

Because the universe was created by, and is operating under the wisdom of God, so many unimaginable things that man can never completely understand, happen every day.

With all these clear evidences, no one can give this excuse on the last judgment day, "I couldn't believe because I didn't know God really existed."

One day, Sir Isaac Newton asked an experienced mechanic to build a sophisticated model of the solar system. An atheist friend of his came to visit him one day and saw the model of the solar system. Without much thought, he turned the crank, and a really amazing thing happened. Each planet on the model began revolving around the sun at different speeds!

The friend couldn't hide his amazement, and said surprisingly, "This is truly an excellent model! Who made it?" How do you think Newton replied? He said, "Oh, nobody made it. It just came together like this by chance."

The friend felt as though Newton was joking with him, and retorted, "What?! You think I'm a fool? How in the world can an intricate model like this just appear out of nowhere?"

At this, Newton answered, "This is just a small model of the real solar system. You're arguing that even a simple model like this can't just come together without a designer or a maker. Then how would you explain to someone who believes that the actual solar system, which is much more complicated and vast, just came to be without a creator?"

This is what Newton wrote in his book, *The Philosophiæ Naturalis Principia Mathematica,* which means "Mathematical Principles of Natural Philosophy" and often called *Principia*, "This most beautiful system of the sun, planets, and comets, could only proceed from the counsel and dominion of an intelligent and powerful Being. ... He [God] is eternal and infinite."

This is why a large number of scientists that study the laws of nature are Christians. The more they study nature and the universe, the more they discover the almighty power of God.

Moreover, through miracles and signs that occur and appear to believers, through God's servants and workers that are loved and recognized by Him, and through the history of man that fulfilled the prophecies from the Bible, God shows us many evidences so that we can believe in Him, the living God.

People Who Recognized God the Creator without Hearing the Gospel

If you look at the history of mankind, you can see that people with good hearts who never once heard the gospel recognized the one and only God the Creator and tried to live in righteousness.

People with impure and confused hearts worshipped many different gods to try to comfort themselves. On the other hand, people with upright and clean hearts only worshipped and served one God, the Creator, even though they didn't know about God.

For example, Admiral Soonshin Yi, who lived during the Chosun Dynasty in Korea, served his country, the King, and his people with all his life. He honored his parents, and during his entire life, he never tried to seek his own benefit, but rather sacrificed himself for others. Although he didn't know about God and our Lord Jesus, he didn't worship shamans, demons or evil spirits, but with a good conscience, he only looked toward the heavens and believed in one creator.

These good people never learned God's word, but you can see that they always tried to lead clean and true lives. God opened a way for these kinds of people to be saved as well, through something called "the Judgment of Conscience." This is God's way of giving salvation to those people from the Old Testament times, or people after Jesus Christ's time who never had the chance to hear the gospel.

In Romans 2:14-15, it is written, *"For when Gentiles who do not have the Law do instinctively the things of the Law, these, not having the Law, are a law to themselves, in that they show the work of the Law written in their hearts, their conscience bearing witness and their thoughts alternately accusing or else defending them."*

When people with a good conscience hear the gospel, they will receive the Lord in their hearts very easily. God allowed these souls to temporarily stay in the 'Upper Grave' so they can enter heaven.
When a person's life ends, his spirit leaves his physical body. The spirit temporarily stays in a place called the "Grave." The Grave is a temporary place where they learn to adapt to the spiritual world before going to their places for eternity. This place is divided into the "Upper Grave," where saved people wait, and the "Lower Grave," where the unsaved souls wait in

torment (Genesis 37:35; Job 7:9; Numbers 16:33; Luke 16).

But in Acts 4:12, it says, *"And there is salvation in no one else; for there is no other name under heaven that has been given among men by which we must be saved."* So, in order to make sure those souls in the Upper Grave have a chance to hear the gospel, Jesus went to the Upper Grave to share the gospel with them.

The Scriptures support this fact. In 1 Peter 3:18-19, it says, *"For Christ also died for sins once for all, the just for the unjust, so that He might bring us to God, having been put to death in the flesh, but made alive in the spirit; in which also He went and made proclamation to the spirits now in prison."* Those "good" souls in the Upper Grave recognized Jesus, received the gospel, and were saved.

So for the people who lived with a good conscience and believed in the one Creator, whether they were from the Old Testament times or they never heard about the gospel or the laws, God of justice looked at the depths of their hearts and opened the door of salvation for them.

Why God Commanded His People Never to Put Any Other Gods before Him

Once in a while, non-believers say, "Christianity requires people to believe in only God. Doesn't this make the religion too inflexible and exclusive?"

There are also people who call themselves believers but depend on palm reading, sorcery, charms and talismans.

God specifically told us not to compromise in this area. He said, "You shall have no other gods before Me." This means we should never associate with and bless false idols or any of God's creations. Nor should we set them as equal to God in any way.

There is only one Creator, who created us, and only He can bless us, and only He can give us life. The false gods and idols that people worship are ultimately from the enemy Satan. They stand in hostility toward God.

The enemy devil tries to confuse people into straying from God. By worshipping things that are false they end up worshipping Satan, and they walk toward their own downfall.

This is why people who claim to believe in God but still worship false idols in their hearts are still under the subjection of the enemy devil. For this reason they continue experiencing pain and sorrow and suffer from sickness, disease, and tribulations.

God is love, and He doesn't want His people to worship false idols and walk toward eternal death. That's why He commands that we are not to have other gods before Him. By worshipping Him alone, we can have eternal life, and we can also receive abundant blessings from Him while living on this earth.

We Must Receive Blessings by Faithfully Depending on God Alone

In 1 Chronicles 16:26, it is written, *"For all the gods of the peoples are idols, but the LORD made the heavens."* If God had never said, "You shall have no other gods before Me," then indecisive people, or even some believers may unknowingly end up worshipping false idols and walk toward eternal death.

We can see this in just the history of the Israelites alone. The Israelites, among all other people, learned about the one and only Creator of the universe, and they experienced His power countless times. But over time, they strayed from God and began worshipping other gods and idols.

They thought the idols of the Gentiles looked good, so they began worshipping those idols side by side with God. As a result, they experienced all kinds of temptations, tribulations, and plagues that the enemy devil and Satan brought upon them. Only when they couldn't withstand the pain and hardship any longer, that's when they would repent and return to God.

The reason why God, who is love, forgave them over and over again and saved them from their troubles was because He didn't want to see them experiencing eternal death as a result of worshipping false idols.

God continually shows us evidence that He is the Creator, the living God, so that we can worship Him, and Him alone. He saved us from sin through His only Son, Jesus Christ, and promised us eternal life and gave us the hope of living eternally in heaven.

God helps us to know and believe that He is the living God by showing us miracles, signs, and wonders through His people, and through the sixty-six books of the Bible, and the history of mankind.

Consequently, we must faithfully worship God, the Creator of the universe who has control over everything in it. As His children, we must bear abundant good fruit by depending solely upon Him.

Chapter 3
The Second Commandment

"You Shall Not Make for Yourself an Idol or Worship It"

Exodus 20:4-6

You shall not make for yourself an idol, or any likeness of what is in heaven above or on the earth beneath or in the water under the earth. You shall not worship them or serve them; for I, the LORD your God, am a jealous God, visiting the iniquity of the fathers on the children, on the third and the fourth generations of those who hate Me, but showing lovingkindness to thousands, to those who love Me and keep My commandments.

"The Lord died on the cross for me. How could I possibly deny the Lord because of the fear of death? I'd rather die ten deaths for the Lord than betray Him and live for a hundred, or even a thousand meaningless years. I have but only one commitment. Please help me overcome the power of death so I don't put my Lord to shame by sparing my own life."

This is the confession of Reverend Ki-Chol Chu, who was martyred after refusing to bow down to a Japanese Shrine. His story is found in the book, *More Than Conquerors: The Story of the Martyrdom of Reverend Ki-Chol Chu*. Without cowering in fear of sword or guns, Reverend Ki-Chol Chu gave up his life to obey God's command of not bowing down to any idols.

"You Shall Not Make for Yourself an Idol or Worship It"

As Christians, it is our duty to love and worship God, and God only. That is why God gave us as the first commandment, "You shall have no other gods before Me." And then to strictly prohibit idol worship, He gave us as the second commandment, "You shall not make for yourself an idol. You shall not worship it or serve it."

At first glance, you may think the first commandment and

the second commandment are the same. But they are set apart as separate commandments because they have different spiritual meanings. The first commandment is a warning against polytheism, and it tells us to worship and love only the one true God.

The second commandment is a lesson against worshipping false idols, and it's also an explanation of the blessings you receive when you worship and love God. Then let's take a closer look at what the word 'idol' means.

The Physical Definition of "Idol"

The word "idol" can be explained in two ways; physical idol and spritual one. First, in the physical sense, an "idol" is "an image or material object created to represent a god that does not have a physical shape to which worship can be addressed."

In other words, an idol can be anything: a tree, a rock, an image of a person, mammals, insects, birds, sea creatures, the sun, moon, stars in the sky, or something formed out of the human imagination that one can make out of steel, silver, gold, or anything else that exists that one can direct homage and worship.

But an idol created by man does not have life, so it can neither answer you, nor give you blessings. If people, who were created in God's image, created another image with their own hands and worshipped it, asking it to bless them, how foolish and funny would that seem to be?

In Isaiah 46:6-7 it says, *"Those who lavish gold from the purse and weigh silver on the scale hire a goldsmith, and he makes it into a god; they bow down, indeed they worship it. They lift it upon the shoulder and carry it; they set it in its place and it stands there. It does not move from its place. Though one may cry to it, it cannot answer; it cannot deliver him from his distress."*

Not only does this Scripture refer to creating an idol and worshipping it; but it also refers to believing in charms against bad luck or carrying out sacrificial rites of bowing down to the dead. Even people's belief in superstitious things and the practice of sorcery falls into this category. People think charms drive away hardships and bring good luck, but this is not true. Spiritually keen people can see that dark, evil spirits are actually attracted to places where charms and idols are, ultimately bringing calamities and tribulations to people in possession of them. Aside from the living God, there is no other god that can bring true blessings to people. Other gods are actually the source of calamities and curses.

Then why do people create idols and worship them? It's because people have a tendency to want to satisfy themselves with things that they can physically see, feel, and touch.

We can see this human psyche in the Israelites as they left Egypt. When they called out to God about their pains and toils from their 400 years of slavery, God appointed Moses as their leader for their exodus from Egypt, and He showed them all kinds of signs and wonders so they could have faith in Him.

When the Pharaoh refused to let them go, God sent ten plagues down on Egypt. And when the Red Sea blocked the Israelites' path, God split the sea in half. Even after experiencing these miracles, while Moses was up in the mountains for forty days to receive the Ten Commandments, his people grew impatient and created an idol and worshipped it. Since God's servant Moses was gone from their sight, they wanted to create something they could see and worship. They created a golden calf and called it the god who led them thus far. They even made sacrifices to it, and they drank, ate, and danced before it. This incident caused the Israelites to experience the great wrath of God.

Because God is spirit, people cannot see Him with their physical eyes, or create a physical figure to represent Him. This is why we should never create an idol and call it "god." And we should never worship it either.

In Deuteronomy 4:23, it says, *"So watch yourselves, that you do not forget the covenant of the LORD your God which He made with you, and make for yourselves a graven image in the form of anything against which the LORD your God has commanded you."* Worshipping some lifeless, powerless idol instead of God, the true Creator, does more harm than good for men.

The Examples of Idol Worship

Some believers may fall into the trap of idol worship without even knowing it. For example, some people may bow to a picture of Jesus, or a statue of the Virgin Mary, or some other forerunner of faith.

A large number of people may not think this is idol worship, but it is a form of idol worship that God does not like. Here is a good example: many people call the Virgin Mary "Holy Mother." But if you study the Bible, you can see that this is clearly wrong.

Jesus was impregnated by the Holy Spirit, not from the sperm and egg of a man and a woman. Therefore, we cannot call the Virgin Mary "mother." For example, today's technology allows doctors to place a man's sperm and a woman's egg into a cutting edge machine that performs artificial insemination. This doesn't mean we can call this machine the "mother" of a child born through this process.

Jesus, being in very nature God the Father, was conceived by the Holy Spirit, and was born through the body of the Virgin Mary so that He could come into this world with a physical body. This is why Jesus calls the Virgin Mary "woman", not "mother" (John 2:4, 19:26). In the Bible, when Mary is referred to as the Lord's "mother," it is only because it is written from the point of view of the disciples who recorded the Bible.

Right before His death, Jesus said to John, "Behold, your mother!" referring to Mary. Here, Jesus was asking John to take care of Mary like his own mother (John 19:27). Jesus made this request because He was trying to console Mary, because He understood the sorrow in her heart, since she served Him from the moment He was conceived by the Holy Spirit, until the moment He reached full maturity by God's power and became independent from her.

Nonetheless, it is not correct to bow to a statue of the Virgin Mary.

A couple of years ago while I was visiting a Middle Eastern country, an influential individual invited me over and showed me an interesting-looking carpet during our conversation. It was a priceless, handcrafted carpet that took years to make. On it was a picture of a black Jesus. From this example, we can see that even the image of Jesus is inconsistent, depending on who the artist or sculptor is. Therefore, if we were to bow down or pray to this image, we would be committing idol worship, which is unacceptable.

What Is Considered "Idol" and What Is Not?

Once in a while there are those who are overly cautious, and they argue that the "cross" found in churches is a type of idol. However, the cross is not an idol. It is a symbol of the gospel that Christians believe in. The reason why believers look upon the cross is to remember the sacred blood of Jesus that was shed for the sin of mankind, and the grace of God that gave us the gospel. The cross can neither be an object of worship nor an idol.

This is the same case with the paintings of Jesus holding a lamb, or *The Last Supper*, or any sculpture where the artist simply wanted to express a thought.

The painting of Jesus holding the lamb shows that He is the good shepherd. The artist did not create this painting for it to become an object of worship. But if someone were to worship it, or bow to it, it becomes an idol.

There are cases where people say, "During the Old Testament times, Moses made an idol." They're referring to the event where the Israelites complained against God so they ended up being bitten by venomous snakes in the desert. When many were dying after being bit by the venomous snakes, Moses made a bronze serpent and put it on a pole. Those who obeyed the word of God and looked upon the bronze serpent lived, and those who didn't look died.

God didn't tell Moses to create the bronze serpent so the people could worship it. He wanted to show the people an illustration of Jesus Christ, who would someday come to save them from the curse they were under, according to the spiritual laws.

Those people, who obeyed God and looked upon the bronze serpent, did not perish for their sins. Likewise, those souls who believe that Jesus Christ died on the cross for their sins and accept Him as their Savior and Lord will not perish because of their sins, but will rather have eternal life.

In 2 Kings 18:4, it says that while the sixteenth king of Judah, Hezekiah, was destroying all the idols in Israel, *"He also broke in pieces the bronze serpent that Moses had made, for until those days the sons of Israel burned incense to it; and it was called Nehushtan."* This reminds people once again that even though the bronze serpent was created as God commanded, it should never become the object of idol worship, because that wasn't God's intention for it.

The Spiritual Meaning of "Idol"

In addition to understanding the word "idol" in the physical sense, we should also understand it in the spiritual sense. The spiritual definition of "idol worship" is "everything that one loves more than God." Idol worship is not just limited to bowing before an image of Buddha or bowing to deceased ancestors.

If out of our own selfish desire we love our parents, husband, wife, or even our children more than God, in the spiritual sense, we are turning these loved ones into "idols." And if we think extremely highly of ourselves and love ourselves, we are turning ourselves into idols.

Of course this does not mean we should love only God and not love anybody else. For example, God tells His children that it is their duty to love their parents in the truth. He also commands them, "Honor your father and your mother." However, if loving our parents brings us to the point of straying away from the truth, then we love our parents more than God and thus have turned them into "idols."

Although our parents gave birth to our physical bodies, because God created the sperm and the egg, or the seeds of life, God is the Father of our spirits. Suppose that some non-Christian parents disapprove of their child going to church on Sundays. If their child, who is a Christian, does not go to church in order to please his parents, then the child loves his parents more than God. This not only saddens God's heart, but it also means that the child doesn't truly love his parents.

If you truly love someone, you will want that person to be saved and gain eternal life. This is true love. So first and foremost, you should keep the Lord's Day holy, and then you should pray for your parents and share the gospel with them as soon as possible. Only then can you say you truly love and honor them.

And vice versa. As a parent, if you truly love your children, you should love God first, and then love your children within God's love. No matter how precious your children may be to you, you cannot protect them from the enemy devil and Satan with your own limited human power. You can neither protect them from sudden accidents, nor cure them from a sickness that is unfamiliar to modern medicine.

But when parents worship God and trust their children in God's hands and love them within God's love, God will protect their children. Not only will He give them spiritual and physical strength, but He will bless them so they become prosperous in all areas of their lives.

This is the same case with the love between husbands and wives. A couple unaware of God's true love will only be able to love each other with fleshly love. They will seek their own benefit at times and thereby argue with one another. And with time, their love for each other may even change.

However, when a couple loves each other within God's love, they will be able to love one another with spiritual love as well.

In this case, the couple will not become angry or offensive to one another, and they will not try to satisfy their own selfish desires. Rather, they will share a love that is unchanging, true, and beautiful.

Loving Something or Someone More than God

Only when we are within God's love and love God the Father first, can we love others with a true love. This is why God tells us to "Love your God first," and "Do not put any other gods before Me." But after hearing this, if you were to say, "I went to church and they told me to only love God and don't love my family members," then you are gravely misunderstanding the spiritual interpretation of His commandment.

If as a believer you break God's commandments or compromise with the world in order to earn material wealth, fame, knowledge, or power, and thereby stray away from walking in the truth, you are making for yourself an idol, in the spiritual sense.

There are also people who don't keep the Lord's Day holy or fail to give their tithes because they love wealth more than God, despite the fact that God promises to bless those who give their tithes.

Oftentimes, teenagers hang up pictures of their favorite

singers, actors, athletes, or instrumentalists in their room, or make bookmarks out of their pictures, or even carry their pictures in their vests or pockets to keep their favorite stars close to their hearts. There are times when these teenagers love these people more than God.

Of course you can love and respect actors, actresses, athletes, etc., who are very good at what they do. But if you love and cherish things of the world to the point that you distance yourself from God, God will not be pleased. In addition, young children who pour all their hearts into certain toys or video games can also end up making these things their "idols."

God's Jealousy out of Love

After giving us a strong commandment against idol worship, God tells us about the blessings for those who obey Him, and the admonition for those who disobey Him.

> "You shall not worship them or serve them; for I, the LORD your God, am a jealous God, visiting the iniquity of the fathers on the children, on the third and the fourth generations of those who hate Me, but showing lovingkindness to thousands, to those who love Me and keep My commandments" (Exodus 20:5-6).

When God says He is a "jealous God" in verse 5, He doesn't

mean He is "jealous" in the same way that people get jealous. Because in actuality, jealousy is not a part of God's character. God uses the word "jealous" here to make it easier for us to understand with our own, human emotions. The jealousy that people feel is of the flesh, foul, unclean, and it hurts the people who are involved.

For example, if a husband's love for his wife changes into a love for another woman and the wife begins to feel jealous of the other woman, the sudden change that occurs in the wife will be a scary sight. The wife will become filled with anger and hatred. She will argue with her husband and announce his shortcomings to all of her acquaintances and he may become a disgrace. At times, the wife may go to the other woman and fight with her, or file a suit against her husband. In this case, where the wife wishes something bad to happen to her husband as a result of her jealousy, her jealousy is not a jealousy out of love, but a jealousy out of hate.

If the woman really loved her husband with spiritual love, instead of feeling jealousy of the flesh, she would first look introspectively at herself, and ask, "Am I in good standing with God? Did I truly love and serve my husband?" And instead of disgracing her husband by calling out his shortcomings to those around her, she would have asked God for wisdom to know how to bring him back to fidelity.

Then what kind of jealousy does God feel? When we don't worship God and we don't live in the truth, God turns His face away from us, which is when we face trials, tribulations, and sicknesses. If this happens, knowing that sicknesses come from sin (John 5:14), believers will repent and try to seek God once again.

As a pastor, I come across church members who experience this from time to time. For example, one church member may be a well-to-do businessman whose business is just booming. With the excuse that he's becoming busier, he loses his focus and ceases praying and doing God's work. He even comes to the point where he misses worshipping God on Sundays.

As a result, God turns His face away from this businessman and the business that was once booming faces a crisis. Only then does he realize his mistake of not living according to God's commands, and repents. God would rather have his loving children face a tough situation for a short time and come to understand His will, become saved, and walk the right path, than fall away forever.

If God didn't feel this jealousy out of love, and instead, just indifferently observed our wrongdoings, not only would we fail to realize our mistakes, but our hearts would become calloused, causing us to sin continuously and ultimately fall to the way of eternal death. So the jealousy that God feels is one out of true love. It is an expression of His great love and desire to renew us and lead us to eternal life.

The Blessings and the Curses that Come from Obedience and Disobedience to the Second Commandment

God is our Creator and Father who sacrificed His one and only Son so that all people can be saved. He is also Sovereign over all people's lives and wants to bless those who worship Him.

And not to worship and adore this God, but rather false idols, is to hate Him. And people who hate God receive His retribution, as it is written that the children will be punished for the sins of the fathers to the third and fourth generations (Exodus 20:5).

As we look around us, we can easily see that families that worshipped idols for generations continue to receive retribution. People from these families may experience malignant and or incurable sicknesses, deformities, mental retardation, demon-possession, suicide, financial hardship, or all kinds of other trials. And if these calamities continued on to the fourth generation, then the family would be totally ruined and irreparable.

But why do you think God said He would punish to the

"third and fourth generation" instead of to the "fourth generation?" This shows God's compassion. He is leaving room for those descendants who repent and seek God, even though their ancestors may have worshipped false idols and were hostile towards God. These people give God a reason to stop the punishment against that household.

But for those whose ancestors were in great hostility toward God and were serious idol worshippers, building up evil, they will face difficulties when trying to accept the Lord. Even if they do accept, it's like they are bound to their ancestors by a spiritual tether, so until they have spiritual victory, they will experience many hardships throughout their spiritual lives. The enemy devil and Satan will interfere in any way he can to keep these people from having faith, in order to drag them into eternal darkness with him.

However, if the descendants, while seeking God's mercy, repent with humble hearts for the sins of their ancestors and try to cast out the sinful natures within themselves, then without a doubt, God will protect them. So on the other hand, when people love God and keep His commandments, God blesses their family to the $1,000^{th}$ generation, allowing them to receive His grace eternally. When we look at how God says He will punish to the third and fourth generation, but He will bless to the $1,000^{th}$ generation, we can clearly see God's love for us.

Now this does not mean you automatically receive abundant blessings just because your ancestors were great servants of God. For example, God called David "a man after My heart," and God promised to bless his descendents (1 Kings 6:12). However, we learn that among David's children, those who turned away from God didn't receive the promised blessings.

When you look at the chronicles of Israelite kings, you can see that those kings who worshipped and served God received the blessings that God promised to David. Under their leadership, their nation thrived and flourished to the point that neighboring nations gave tribute to them. However, the kings who turned away from God and sinned against Him experienced many hardships during their lifetime.

Only when a person loves God and tries to live in the truth without tainting himself with idols can he receive all the blessings that his ancestors may have built up for him.

So when we cast away all the spiritual and physical idols that are detestable to God from our lives and put Him first, we too can receive the abundant blessings that God promises to all His faithful servants and their generations thereafter.

Chapter 4
The Third Commandment

"You Shall Not Take the Name of the LORD Your God in Vain"

Exodus 20:7

You shall not take the name of the LORD your God in vain, for the LORD will not leave him unpunished who takes His name in vain.

It's easy to see that the Israelites truly cherished God's words, from the way they recorded the Bible or even read from it.

Before printing was invented, people had to write the Bible by hand. And every time the word "Jehovah" had to be written, the writer would wash his body several times and would even change the brush he was writing with, because the name was so holy. And whenever the writer made a mistake, he had to cut out that section and put new writing over it. But if "Jehovah" happened to be misprinted, he would start examining everything completely over from the beginning.

Also at one time, when the Israelites read from the Bible, they didn't read the name "Jehovah" out loud. Instead, they read it as "Adonai," meaning "My Lord," because they considered God's name too holy to be read.

Because the name "Jehovah" is a name representing God, they believed it was also a representation of God's glorious and sovereign character. To them, the name stood for the One who is the Almighty Creator.

"You Shall Not Take the Name of the LORD Your God in Vain"

Some people don't even remember that there is such a

commandment in the Ten Commandments. Even among believers, there are people who don't hold God's name in high esteem, and end up misusing His name.

To "misuse" means to use something in a wrong or improper way. And to misuse God's name is to use God's holy name in an incorrect, unholy, or untruthful way.

For example, if someone speaks his own mind and claims he is speaking God's words, or if he acts however he wants, and claims he is acting according to God's will, he is misusing His name. Using God's name to make an untruthful oath, joking around with God's name, etc., are all examples of taking God's name in vain.

Another common way people take God's name in vain is when those, who don't even seek Him, face a distressing situation and resentfully say, "God is so indifferent!" or, "If God was truly alive, how can He let this happen?!"

How could God possibly call us sinless if we, the creation, misuse our own Creator's name, the Creator who deserves all glory and honor? This is why we must honor God and try to live in the truth by constantly examining ourselves with discretion to make sure that we're not exhibiting insolence or disrespect before God.

So why is taking God's name in vain a sin?

First of All, Misusing God's Name Is a Sign that We Do Not Believe in Him.

Even among philosophers who claim to study the meaning of life and the existence of the universe, there are those people who say, "God is dead." And even some ordinary people recklessly say, "There is no God."

Once, a Russian astronaut said, "I went to outer space, and God was nowhere to be seen." But as an astronaut, he should have known better than anyone else that the area that he explored was just a tiny part of the vast universe. How foolish it is for the astronaut to say that God, the Creator of the entire universe, does not exist merely because he couldn't see God with his eyes within the relatively insignificant portion of space that he visited!

Psalm 53:1 reads, *"The fool has said in his heart, 'There is no God.' They are corrupt, and have committed abominable injustice; there is no one who does good."* A person who sees the universe with a humble heart can discover a myriad of evidence pointing to God the Creator (Romans 1:20).

God gave everyone a chance to believe in Him. Before Jesus Christ, in the Old Testament times, God touched the heart of good people so they could feel the living God. After Jesus Christ, now, in the New Testament times, God continues to knock on the door of people's hearts in many different ways so people may come to know Him.

That is why good people open their hearts and accept Jesus Christ and become saved, regardless of how they heard the gospel. God allows those who earnestly seek Him to experience His presence through a strong impression on their heart during prayer, through visions, or spiritual dreams.

Once I heard the testimony of one of our church members, and I couldn't help but be amazed. One night, this woman's mother, who had passed away from stomach cancer, came to her in a dream, saying, "If I had met Dr. Jaerock Lee, Senior Pastor of Manmin Central Church, I would have been cured…" This woman was already familiar with Manmin Central Church, but through this experience, her whole family ended up registering at the church and her only son was cured of epilepsy.

There are still people who continue to deny God's existence, despite the fact that He is showing us His existence through many ways. This is because their hearts are wicked and foolish. If these people continue to harden their hearts against God, speaking carelessly about Him without even believing in Him, how can He call them sinless?

God, who even numbers the very hairs of our heads, is watching our every action with fiery eyes. If people believed this fact, in no way would they ever misuse God's name. Some people may seem like they believe, but because they don't believe from the center of their hearts, they may take His name in vain. And this becomes a sin before God.

Secondly, Misusing God's Name Is to Disregard God.

If we disregard God, then it means we do not respect Him. If we dare disrespect God, the Creator, and we cannot say we are without sin.

Psalm 96:4 says, *"For great is the LORD and greatly to be praised; He is to be feared above all gods."* In 1 Timothy 6:16, it says, *"Who [God] alone possesses immortality and dwells in unapproachable light, whom no man has seen or can see. To Him be honor and eternal dominion! Amen."*

Exodus 33:20 reads, *"But He said, 'You cannot see My face, for no man can see Me and live!'"* God the Creator is so great and mighty that we, the creation, cannot irreverently look at Him whenever we please.

That is why in the olden times, people with a good conscience, even though they didn't know God, referred to heaven with words of respect. For example, in Korea, people would use the honorific form, when talking about heaven or the weather, to show respect for the Creator. They might not have known the Jehovah God, but they knew that an almighty Creator of the universe was sending them the things that they needed, like rain, from heaven above. So they wanted to show

Him respect with their words.

Most people use words that show respect and do not misuse the names of their parents or people they truly respect from their hearts. So if we're talking about God the Creator of the universe and Giver of life, shouldn't we refer to Him with the holiest of attitudes and words of highest respect?

Unfortunately, there are some people today who call themselves believers and yet don't show respect to God, let alone take Him seriously. For example, they make jokes using God's name or quote the words of the Bible in a careless way. Since the Bible says, "The Word was God," (John 1:1) if we disrespect the words of the Bible, it's just like disrespecting God.

Another way of disrespecting God is by lying with His name. An example of this would be if a person talks about something conjured up from his own mind and says, "This is the voice of God," or "This is something led by the Holy Spirit." If we consider using an elderly person's name in an inappropriate manner as rude and impolite, then how much more should we caution ourselves about using God's name in that way?

The almighty God knows the heart and thoughts of all living creatures like the palm of His hand. And He knows whether their every action is motivated by evil or good. With eyes like fire, God watches every person's life, and He will judge each person according to his actions. If a person truly believes this, he will surely not misuse God's name or commit the sin of being impudent towards Him.

One more thing we should remember is that people who truly love God should not only be cautious when using God's name, but also when dealing with all things that are related to Him. People who truly love God also treat the church building and church's property even more carefully than their own. And they are very careful when dealing with money that belongs to the church, no matter how small the amount.

If you accidentally broke a cup, or a mirror, or a window of a church, would you pretend it never happened and forget about it? No matter how small they are, things that are specifically set apart for God and His ministry should never be neglected or mistreated.

We must also be careful that we don't judge or belittle a person of God, or an event led by the Holy Spirit, because they are directly related to God.

Although Saul did a lot of evil against David and was a great threat to him, David spared Saul's life to the end, for the sole reason that Saul was once a king anointed by God (1 Samuel 26:23). Likewise, a person who loves and respects God will be very careful when dealing with everything that's related to God.

Thirdly, Misusing God's Name Is to Lie with His Name.

If you look at the Old Testament, there are some false prophets embedded in the history of Israel. These false prophets confused the people by giving them information that they claimed to be from God but actually weren't.

In Deuteronomy 18:20, God gives a stern warning against people like these. He says, *"But the prophet who speaks a word presumptuously in My name which I have not commanded him to speak, or which he speaks in the name of other gods, that prophet shall die."* If someone lies using God's name, the punishment for their action is death.

Revelations 21:8 says, *"But for the cowardly and unbelieving and abominable and murderers and immoral persons and sorcerers and idolaters and all liars, their part will be in the lake that burns with fire and brimstone, which is the second death."*

If there is a second death, that means there is a first death. This refers to people dying in this world without believing in God. These people will go to the Lower Grave, where they will receive the painful punishment for their sins. On the other hand, those who are saved will be like kings for a thousand years during the Millennium Kingdom on this earth after meeting the Lord Jesus Christ in the air at His second coming.

After the Millennium Kingdom, there will be the Judgment of the Great White Throne where all people will be judged and receive either spiritual rewards or punishments, according to their actions. At this time, those souls who weren't saved will also resurrect to face this judgment, and each, according to the weight of their sins, will enter either the lake of fire or burning sulfur. This is what is known as the second death.

The Bible says that all liars will experience the second death. Here, liars refer to anyone who lies using God's name. This is not only limited to false prophets; but also those people who swear an oath by God's name and break the oath, since this is the same as lying with His name and thus a misuse of His name. In Leviticus 19:12, God says, *"'You shall not swear falsely by My name, so as to profane the name of your God; I am the LORD.'"*

But there are believers who sometimes lie using God's name. For example they might say, "While I was praying, I heard the voice of the Holy Spirit. I believe it was God's doing," even though God had nothing to do with it. Or, they might see something happening and even though it is not for certain, they say, "God made this happen." It's fine if it really is God's work, but it becomes a problem when it isn't the work of the Holy Spirit and they just habitually say it is.

Of course as a child of God we should always listen for the

Holy Spirit's voice and receive His guidance. But it's important to know that just because you are a saved child of God, it doesn't mean that you can always hear the voice of the Holy Spirit. According to how much a person is able to empty himself of sins and becomes filled with the truth, he will be able to hear the Holy Spirit's voice that much more clearly. And so if a person does not live in the truth and compromises with the world, he cannot clearly hear the voice of the Holy Spirit.

If someone is full of untruth and he boisterously and ostentatiously label the products of his own fleshly thinking as the work of the Holy Spirit, he is not only lying before other people; he is also lying before God. Even if he really did hear the voice of the Holy Spirit, until he hears His voice 100 percent, he should make the effort to be discreet. Therefore we must refrain from recklessly calling something a work of the Holy Spirit and we should also listen to such claims with great caution.

The same rule applies to dreams, visions, and other spiritual experiences. Some dreams are given by God, but some dreams may occur as a result of an individual's strong desire or worry. And some dreams may even be the work of Satan, so one should never jump to say, "This dream was given by God," because that would be an improper thing to do before God.

There are times when people blame God for the tribulations or hardships that are actually caused by Satan as a result of their own sins. And there are times when people carelessly place God's name on things out of habit. When things seem to be going their way, they say, "God blessed me." Then when hardships come, they say, "Oh, God closed the door on that." Some may give a confession of faith, but it's important to know that there is a big difference between a confession that is from a true heart and a confession from a flippant and boasting heart.

Proverbs 3:6 says, *"In all your ways acknowledge Him, and He will make your paths straight."* But this does not mean to always label everything with God's holy name. Rather, someone who acknowledges God in all his ways will try to live in the truth at all times and thus be more cautious about using God's name. And when he does need to use it, he will do so with a faithful and discreet heart.

Therefore if we don't want to commit the sin of misusing God's name, we should strive to meditate on His word day and night, be watchful in prayer, and be filled with the Holy Spirit. Only when we do this can we clearly hear the voice of the Holy Spirit and act in righteousness, according to His guidance.

Always Revere Him, Be Considered Noble

God is accurate and meticulous. And so every single word that He uses in the Bible is right and proper. When you look at how He addresses believers, you can see that God uses just the right words for the situation. For example, calling someone "Brother," and calling someone "My beloved," carries a totally different tone and meaning. Sometimes God addresses people as "Fathers," or "Young men," or "Children," etc., using the appropriate words that carry just the right definition, depending on the addressee's measure of faith (1 Corinthians 1:10; 1 John 2:12-13, 3:21-22).

The same applies to the names for the Holy Trinity. We see a variety of names used for the Trinity: "LORD God, Jehovah, God the Father, the Messiah, Lord Jesus, Jesus Christ, Lamb, Spirit of the Lord, Spirit of God, Sacred Spirit, Spirit of holiness, Holy Spirit, Spirit (Genesis 2:4; 1 Chronicles 28:12; Psalm 104:30; John 1:41; Romans 1:4).

Especially in the New Testament, before the time Jesus Christ took up the cross, He is called, "Jesus, Teacher, Son of Man," but after He died and resurrected, He is called, "Jesus Christ, the Lord Jesus Christ, Jesus Christ of Nazareth" (1 Timothy 6:14; Acts 3:6).

Before He was crucified, He hadn't completed His mission as the Savior yet, so He was called "Jesus," which means "The one who will save His people from their sins" (Matthew 1:21). But after He completed His mission, He was called "Christ," which carries the meaning of "Savior."

God, who is perfect, also wants us to be correct and perfect with our words and our actions too. Therefore whenever we speak God's holy name, we must express it all the more correctly. That is why God says in the latter part of 1 Samuel 2:30, *"For those who honor Me I will honor, and those who despise Me will be lightly esteemed."*

So if we truly regard God with great respect from the center of our hearts, we will never make the mistake of misusing His name, and we will fear Him at all times. So I pray that you can always be on the alert in prayer, and watchful of your heart, so that the life you lead gives glory to God.

Chapter 5
The Fourth Commandment

"Remember the Sabbath Day, to Keep It Holy"

Exodus 20:8-11

Remember the sabbath day, to keep it holy. Six days you shall labor and do all your work, but the seventh day is a sabbath of the LORD your God; in it you shall not do any work, you or your son or your daughter, your male or your female servant or your cattle or your sojourner who stays with you. For in six days the LORD made the heavens and the earth, the sea and all that is in them, and rested on the seventh day; therefore the LORD blessed the sabbath day and made it holy.

If you accepted Christ and became a child of God, the first things you need to do are to worship God every Sunday and give whole tithes. As giving your whole tithes and offerings shows your faith in God's authority over all physical and material things, and keeping the Sabbath day holy shows your faith in God's authority over all spiritual things. (See Ezekiel 20:11-12).

When you act with faith, acknowledging God's spiritual and physical authority, you will receive God's protection from disasters, temptations, and distress. Offering tithes will be discussed in more detail in chapter 8, so this chapter will focus specifically on keeping the Sabbath day holy.

Why Sunday Became the Sabbath Day

The day of rest dedicated to God is called the "Sabbath" day. This originated from when God, the Creator, formed the universe and man in six days and then rested on the seventh day (Genesis 2:1-3). God blessed this day and made it holy, making man rest on this day also.

In the Old Testament times, the Sabbath day was actually Saturday. And even today, Jews keep Saturday as the Sabbath day. But as we entered the New Testament times, Sunday became the Sabbath day and we began calling this day the

"Lord's Day." John 1:17 says, *"For the Law was given through Moses; grace and truth were realized through Jesus Christ."* And Matthew 12:8 says, *"For the Son of Man is Lord of the Sabbath."* And this is exactly what happened.

Why, then, did the Sabbath day change from Saturday to Sunday? This is because the day that all mankind is able to have true rest through Jesus Christ is Sunday.

Because of the disobedience of the first man, Adam, all mankind became slaves to sin and did not have a true Sabbath. Man could only eat by the sweat of his brow and had to suffer and experience tears of sorrow, sickness, and death. This is why Jesus came to this world in the form of human flesh and was crucified, in order to pay for all of mankind's sins. He died and rose again on the third day, conquering death and becoming the firstfruits of resurrection.

So Jesus resolved the issue of sin and gave true Sabbath to all of mankind, at early dawn on Sunday, the first day after the Sabbath day. For this reason, in the New Testament times, Sunday—the day Jesus Christ completed the way of salvation for all mankind—became the Sabbath day.

Jesus Christ, the Lord of the Sabbath

The Lord's disciples also designated Sunday as the Sabbath day, understanding the spiritual significance of the Sabbath day. Acts 20:7 reads, *"On the first day of the week, when we were gathered together to break bread,"* and 1 Corinthians 16:2 reads, *"On the first day of every week each one of you is to put aside and save, as he may prosper, so that no collections be made when I come."*

God knew this change of the Sabbath day was going to happen, so He alluded to this in the Old Testament when He said to Moses, *"Speak to the sons of Israel and say to them, 'When you enter the land which I am going to give to you and reap its harvest, then you shall bring in the sheaf of the first fruits of your harvest to the priest. He shall wave the sheaf before the LORD for you to be accepted; on the day after the sabbath the priest shall wave it. Now on the day when you wave the sheaf, you shall offer a male lamb one year old without defect for a burnt offering to the LORD'"* (Leviticus 23:10-12).

God was telling the Israelites that once they entered the land of Canaan, they would sacrifice their first harvested grain on the day after the Sabbath day. The first harvested grain symbolizes the Lord who became the firstfruits of resurrection. And the one year old lamb without defect also symbolizes Jesus Christ, the Lamb of God.

These verses show that on Sunday, the day after the

Sabbath, Jesus, who became the peace offering and firstfruits of the resurrection, would give resurrection and true Sabbath to all those who believe in Him.

For this reason, Sunday, the day that Jesus Christ resurrected, became a day of true joy and thanksgiving; a day when new life was conceived and the way to eternal life was opened; and the day that true Sabbath could finally take place.

"Remember the Sabbath Day, to Keep It Holy"

So why has God made the Sabbath day holy and why does He tell His people to keep it holy?
This is because, although we may be living in a flesh-driven world, God wanted us to remember the things of the spiritual world as well. He wanted to make sure our hope isn't solely for the perishable things of this world. He wanted us to remember the Master and Creator of the universe and have hope in the true and eternal Sabbath of His kingdom.

Exodus chapter 20 verses 9-10 says, *"Six days you shall labor and do all your work, but the seventh day is a sabbath of the LORD your God; in it you shall not do any work, you or your son or your daughter, your male or your female servant or your cattle or your sojourner who stays with you."* This means that no one should work on the Sabbath day. This includes you, your servants, your animals, and any visitor in your house.

This is why the orthodox Jewish people aren't allowed to prepare food, move heavy objects, or travel far distances on the Sabbath day. It is because all of these activities are considered labor and thus they are not in compliance with the rules of the Sabbath. However, these restrictions were made by people and were passed down from elders to the next; therefore they are not God's rules.

For example, when the Jews were looking for a reason to bring accusation against Jesus, they saw a man with a shriveled hand and they asked Jesus, "Is it lawful to heal on the Sabbath?" They even considered healing a sick person on the Sabbath day as "labor" and thus unlawful.

To this, Jesus said to them, *"What man is there among you who has a sheep, and if it falls into a pit on the Sabbath, will he not take hold of it and lift it out? How much more valuable then is a man than a sheep! So then, it is lawful to do good on the Sabbath"* (Matthew 12:11-12).

Keeping the Sabbath that God is talking about isn't simply abstaining from any sort of work. When non-believers rest from work and stay home, or go out to enjoy recreational activities, this is a physical rest from work. This is not considered a "sabbath," because this does not give us true life. We must first understand the spiritual meaning of the "Sabbath," in order for us to keep it holy and be blessed, the way God first intended for us.

What God wants us to do on this day is not to take a physical rest, but a spiritual rest. Isaiah 58:13-14 explains that on the Sabbath day, people should keep themselves from doing as they please, going their own way, speaking idle words, or enjoying the joys of the world. Instead, they should keep the day holy.

On the Sabbath day, one should not become tangled with the events of the world, but go to church, which is the body of the Lord; take in the bread of life, which is the word of God; have fellowship with the Lord through prayer and praise; and take a spiritual rest in the Lord. Through fellowship believers should share God's grace with each other and help to build up one another's faith. When we take a spiritual rest like this, God matures our faith and makes our soul prosper.

So what, exactly, should be done to keep the Sabbath day holy?

First, We Must Desire the Blessings of the Sabbath Day and Prepare Ourselves to Be Clean Vessels.

The Sabbath day is a day that God set apart as holy, and it is a joyful day when we can receive blessings from God. The latter part of Exodus 20:11 says, *"Therefore the LORD blessed the sabbath day and made it holy,"* and Isaiah 58:13 says, *"And call the sabbath a delight, the holy day of the LORD honorable, and honor it."*

Even today, since Israelites keep Saturday as the Sabbath day, as in the Old Testament times, they begin preparing for the Sabbath a day in advance. They have all the food prepared, and if they were to be working away from home, they would arrange to rush home no later than Friday evening.

We too, must prepare our hearts for the Sabbath before Sunday. Every week, we should always be awake in prayer before Sunday comes and try to live in the truth at all times so that we do not build up any barriers of sin between God and ourselves.

So keeping the Sabbath day holy doesn't mean giving God just that single day. It means living the whole week in accordance with God's words. And so, if we did anything during the week that might be unacceptable to God, we should repent and prepare for Sunday with a clean heart.

And when coming to Sunday worship, we need to come before God with a thankful heart. We must come before Him with a joyful and anticipating heart, like a bride waiting for her groom. With this kind of attitude, we may physically prepare ourselves by taking a bath, and maybe even go to the barber or salon to make sure we appear neat and kempt.

We may even want to clean the house as well. We should

also have a neat and clean outfit picked out ahead of time, to wear to church. We should not get involved in any worldly affairs late Saturday night that carry over into Sunday. We should refrain from activity that may hinder the worship we offer to God on Sunday. Also, we need to try to guard our hearts against getting irritable, angry, or upset, so that we can worship God in spirit and in truth.

So with an exciting and loving heart, we should anticipate Sunday and prepare ourselves to be a vessel worthy of receiving God's grace. This will enable us to experience a spiritual Sabbath in the Lord.

Secondly, We Should Give All Day Sunday Wholly to God

Even among believers, there are people who give God only the one worship service on Sunday morning, and then skip the evening worship. They do it to either to rest, for recreational activity, or to take care of other business. If we really want to properly keep the Sabbath holy with a God-fearing heart, we must keep the whole day holy. The reason why we skip afternoon services to do a variety of things is because we let our hearts follow what pleases the flesh, and then we pursue worldly things.

With this kind of attitude, it's very easy to get distracted with other thoughts during the morning service. And even though we may have come to church, we won't be able to give God true worship. During the worship, our minds might be filled with thoughts such as, "I'm going to go home and relax as soon as this service is over," or "Ooh, won't it be so fun to see my friends after church," or "I'd better hurry and open the store as soon as this is over." All kinds of thoughts will go in and out of our minds and we won't be able to focus on the message, or we may even become sleepy and tired during the worship.

Of course for new believers, since their faith is young, they may become easily distracted, or because they are physically very tired, they may become sleepy. Since God knows everyone's measure of faith and looks at the center of everyone's heart, He will be merciful to them. But if someone who is supposed to have considerable measure of faith habitually becomes distracted and falls asleep during worship, he is simply being disrespectful to God.

Keeping the Sabbath day holy doesn't mean just being physically inside the church on Sunday. It means keeping the center of our heart and our attention focused on God. Only when we worship God properly all day on Sunday in spirit and in truth will He joyfully receive the pleasing aroma of our hearts in worship.

In order to keep the Sabbath day holy, it's also important

how you spend the hours outside of worship, on Sundays. We should not think, "Since I attended worship, I've done everything I need to do." After worship, we need to have fellowship with other believers and serve God's kingdom by cleaning the church, or directing traffic in the church parking lot, or doing other volunteer work in the church.

And after the day is over and we go home to rest, we should refrain from recreational activities with the sole purpose of pleasing oneself. Instead, we should meditate on the message we heard that day, or spend time talking and sharing with our family about God's grace and truth. It would be a good idea to keep the television off, but if we do happen to watch, we should try to avoid certain kinds of shows that could trigger our lust or that could make us seek worldly pleasure. Instead turn to programs that are wholesome, clean, and even better yet, faith-based.

When we show God that we're trying our best to please Him, even with the little things, God, who looks at the center of each of our hearts, will receive our worship with joy, fill us with the fullness of the Holy Spirit, and bless us so that we can have a true rest.

Thirdly, We Must Not Do Worldly Work.

Nehemiah, the governor of Israel under King Artaxerxes, King of Persia, understanding God's will, not only rebuilt walls of the city of Jerusalem but also made sure the people kept the

Sabbath day holy.

That is why he prohibited working or selling on the Sabbath day, and he even chased away the people who slept outside the city walls who were waiting there to conduct business on the day after the Sabbath day.

In Nehemiah 13:17-18, Nehemiah warns his people, *"What is this evil thing you are doing, by profaning the sabbath day? Did not your fathers do the same, so that our God brought on us and on this city all this trouble?"* What Nehemiah is saying is that doing business on the Sabbath day violates the Sabbath and stirs up God's wrath.

Whoever violates the Sabbath does not acknowledge God's authority and does not believe in His promise to bless those who keep the Sabbath day holy. That is why God, who is just, cannot protect them, and calamity is bound to fall upon them.

God still commands the same thing to all of us today. He tells us to work hard for six days, and then take a rest on the seventh day. And if we remember the Sabbath day by keeping it holy, then God will not only give us enough to make up for the profit we could have made by working on the seventh day, but He'll bless us to the point that our 'storehouses' overflow.

If you look at Exodus chapter 16, you'll see that while God provided the Israelites with manna and quail every day, on the sixth day, He poured down double the portion He sent on the other days, so they could prepare for the Sabbath day. Among the Israelites, there were some who, out of selfishness, went out to collect manna on the Sabbath day but returned empty-handed.

The same spiritual law applies to us today. If a child of God does not keep the Sabbath day holy and decides to work on the Sabbath day, he may reap a short-term profit, but in the long run, for this reason and that, he will actually experience a long-term loss.

The truth of the matter is, even if it seems like you're making a profit at the time, without God's protection, you're bound to experience some unforeseen trouble. For instance, you may get into an accident, or become ill, etc., which will end up being a greater loss in the end than any profit made.

On the contrary, if you remember the Sabbath day to keep it holy, God will watch over you for the rest of the week and lead you toward prosperity. The Holy Spirit will guard you with His pillars of fire, and protect you from sicknesses. He will bless you and your business, your workplace, and everywhere else you may go.

This is why God made this commandment one of the Ten Commandments. He even set up as a serious punishment, the stoning of people who were caught working on the Sabbath day, so His people would remember and not forget the importance of the Sabbath day and not go down the path to eternal death (Numbers Chapter 15).

From the moment I accepted Christ into my life, I made certain to remember the Sabbath and keep it holy. Before I planted our church, I ran a bookstore. On Sundays, many people came to the store wanting to borrow or return books. And every time this happened, I said, "Today is the Lord's Day, so the store is closed," and I did not do business on that day. As a result, instead of experiencing a loss, God actually poured out so much blessing on the six days that we worked, that we never even had to think about working on Sundays ever again!

When Working or Doing Business on the Sabbath Day Is Permitted

When you look at the Bible, there were cases where working or doing business on the Sabbath day was permitted. These are the cases where the work is necessary for doing the Lord's work or for doing good works, such as saving people's lives.

Matthew 12:5-8 says, *"Or have you not read in the Law, that on the Sabbath the priests in the temple break the Sabbath and are innocent? But I say to you that something greater than the temple is here. But if you had known what this means, 'I desire compassion, and not a sacrifice,' you would not have condemned the innocent. For the Son of Man is Lord of the Sabbath."*

When priests slaughter animals for burnt offering on the Sabbath day, it is not considered labor. So any work done for the Lord on the Lord's Day is not considered transgressing the Sabbath, since He is the Lord of the Sabbath.

For example, if the church wants to provide the choir and teachers with a meal for working hard at church all day, but the church does not have a cafeteria or the right facility in which to do this, then it is permissible for the church to buy food for them elsewhere. This is because the Lord of the Sabbath is Jesus Christ, and buying the food in this case is for doing the Lord's work. Of course it would be more ideal if the food could be prepared within the church.

When bookstores are opened on Sundays within the church, it is not considered desecrating the Sabbath because the items being sold by the church bookstores are not considered things of the world but they are only items that give life to the believers in the Lord. They include Bibles, Hymnals, recordings of sermons, and other church related things. Also, the vending machines and canteens within the church are also allowed because they help believers in the church on the Sabbath day. The profit from these sales is used for supporting missions and good will organizations, so they are different from the profit from secular sales that go on outside the church.

God does not consider some kinds of work on the Sabbath

to be in violation of the Sabbath such as jobs in the military, police forces, hospitals, etc. These are jobs in which the work is done to protect and save lives and to do good works. However, even if you fall into this category, you should try to focus on God, even if it means just in your heart. Your heart should be willing to appeal to your superior to change your day off, if that's possible, in order to keep the Sabbath.

What about believers who hold their wedding ceremonies on Sunday? If they claim to believe in God and they have their wedding ceremony on the Lord's Day, it shows that their faith is very young. But if someone like this decides to have his wedding on Sunday and nobody from his church attends the wedding, he may feel offended and slide in his walk of faith. So in this case, church members may attend the wedding ceremony after the Sunday worship service.

It is to show consideration for the individuals getting married and to prevent hurt feeling and slipping in their believing lives. However, after the ceremony it is not acceptable for you to stay at the reception that is intended for guests to enjoy themselves.

Aside from these cases, there may be many more questions about the Sabbath day. But, once you begin to understand God's heart you can easily find the answer to those questions. When you cast off all the evil from your heart, you can then worship God with all your heart. You can act out of sincere love toward other souls instead of judging them with man-made rules and regulations like the Sadducees and the Pharisees. You can enjoy a true Sabbath in the Lord without desecrating the Lord's Day. Then, you will know God's will in all situations. You will know what to do by the guidance of the Holy Spirit and you will always be able to enjoy freedom by living in the truth.

God is love, so if His children obey His commandments and do what pleases Him, He will give them whatever they ask (1 John 3:21-22). He will not only shower us with His grace, but He will also bless us so we can be prosperous and successful in all areas of our lives. At the end of our lives He will lead us to the best dwelling place of heaven.

He has prepared heaven for us so that, just as a bride and groom share love and happiness together, we can share love and happiness eternally in heaven with our Lord. This is the true Sabbath that God has in store for us. So I pray that your faith will mature and become greater with each passing day, as you remember the Sabbath day by keeping it complete and holy.

Chapter 6
The Fifth Commandment

"Honor Your Father and Your Mother"

Exodus 20:12

Honor your father and your mother, that your days may be prolonged in the land which the LORD your God gives you.

One cold winter, when the streets of Korea were full of suffering refugees from the devastation of the Korean War, there was a woman getting ready to give birth. She had miles to go before reaching her planned destination, but as her contractions grew stronger and more frequent, she carefully climbed under an abandoned bridge. Laying on the cold, freezing ground, she endured the pains of childbirth alone and brought into the world a small child. Then she covered the blood-covered baby with her own clothes and held him in her bosom.

A few moments later, an American soldier who was passing by the bridge heard a baby's cry. Following the crying sound, he climbed under the bridge and found a dead, frozen, naked woman hunched over a crying baby covered in layers of clothing. Like the woman in this story, parents love their children to the point of easily and selflessly giving up their own life for them. Then how much greater do you think is God's unconditional love for us?

"Honor Your Father and Your Mother"

To "Honor your father and your mother" means to obey the will of your parents, and to serve them with sincere respect and courtesy. Our parents gave birth to us and raised us. If our parents didn't exist, then we wouldn't exist. So even if God hadn't made this commandment one of the Ten Commandments, people with good hearts would honor their parents anyway.

God gives us this commandment, "Honor your father and your mother," because as He mentions in Ephesians 6:1, *"Children, obey your parents in the Lord, for this is right,"* He wants us to honor our parents according to His word. If you happen to disobey God's word in order to please your parents, then this is not truly honoring your parents.

For example, if you're about to go to church on Sunday and your parents say, "Don't go to church today. Let's have some family time," then what should we do? If you obey your parents in order to please them, it's not really honoring them. It's violating the Sabbath day and going towards eternal darkness together with your parents.

Even if you obey and serve them well in the flesh, since this is, spiritually, the way to eternal Hell, how can you say you truly love your parents? You must first act according to God's will, and then try to move your parents' hearts so you can all go to heaven together. This is truly honoring them.

In 2 Chronicles 15:16, it says, *"He also removed Maacah, the mother of King Asa, from the position of queen mother, because she had made a horrid image as an Asherah, and Asa cut down her horrid image, crushed it and burned it at the brook Kidron."*

If the queen of one nation worships idols, she is being hostile toward God and walking toward eternal condemnation. Not only that, she is endangering her subjects by making them commit acts of idol worship and fall into the same eternal condemnation with her. That is why, even though Maacah was his mother, Asa didn't try to please her by obeying her, but instead he deposed her from her position as queen mother so that she could repent of her wrongdoing before God and the people could wake up and do the same.

But King Asa's deposal of his mother from her position as queen didn't mean he stopped fulfilling his duty as her son. As much as he loved her soul, he continued to respect and honor her as his mother.

In order to say, "I truly honored my parents," we must help unbelieving parents to receive salvation and go to heaven. If our parents are already believers, we must help them to enter into the best dwelling place of heaven. At the same time, we should also try to serve and please them as much as we can within God's truth, while living here on earth.

God Is the Father of Our Spirits

"Honor your father and your mother" ultimately means

the same as "Obey God's commandments and honor Him." If someone truly honors God in the depth of his hearts, he will also honor his parents. And likewise, if someone sincerely serves his parents, he will sincerely serve God as well. But the truth of the matter is, when it comes to priority, God should be first.

For example, in many cultures if a father tells his son, "Go to the east," then the son will obey and go to the east. But if at this time, his grandfather says, "No, don't go to the east. Go to the west." Then it's more correct for the son to tell his father, "Grandfather told me to go to the west," and then go to the west.

If the father truly honors his own father, he won't get angry merely because his son obeyed his grandfather instead of himself. This act of obeying one's elders, according to their generation level, applies to our relationship with God as well.

God is the One who created and gave life to our father, grandfather, and all of our ancestors. A person is created by the union of a sperm and an egg. But the One who gives man the basic seed of life is God.

Our visible bodies are nothing more than temporary tents we use for the short time that we live here on this earth. After God, the true master of each of us is the spirit within us. No matter how smart and knowledgeable mankind becomes, no one can clone a person's spirit. And even if man is able to clone human cells and create a human form, unless God gives that form a spirit, we cannot call the form a human being.

Therefore the true Father of our spirit is God. Knowing this fact, we should do our best to serve and honor our physical parents, but we should love, serve, and honor God even more, because He is the originator and giver of life itself.

So a parent who understands this will never think, "I gave birth to my child, so I can do whatever I want with him." As written in Psalm 127:3, *"Behold, children are a gift of the LORD, the fruit of the womb is a reward,"* parents with faith will consider their child a God-given enterprise and a priceless soul who should be nurtured according to God's will and not their own.

How to Honor God, the Father of Our Spirits

Then what should we do in order to honor God, the Father of our spirits?

If you truly honor your parents, you should obey them and try to bring joy and comfort to their hearts. In the same way, if you truly want to honor God, you should love Him and obey His commands.

As it is written in 1 John 5:3, *"For this is the love of God, that we keep His commandments; and His commandments are not burdensome,"* if you truly love God, then obeying His commands should be enjoyable.

The commands of God are within the words recorded in the sixty-six books of the Bible. Namely, there are words like "Love, forgive, make peace, serve, pray," etc., where God tells us to do something, and then there are words like "Do not hate, do not condemn, do not be conceited," etc., where God tells us not to do something. There are also words like "Throw away even the mere form of sin," etc., where God tells us to cast out something from our lives, and words like "Keep the Sabbath day holy," etc., where God tells us to keep something.

Only when we act according to the commands that are recorded in the Bible and become a fragrant aroma to God as a Christian, can we say that we're truly honoring God the Father.

It's easy to see that people who love and honor God love and honor their physical parents as well. This is because God's commandments already include honoring our parents and loving our brothers.

Do you by any chance love God and do your best to serve Him at church, but neglect your parents at home in any way? Are you ever humble and amiable in front of your brothers and sisters at church but at times become rude and insulting to your family at home? Do you confront your elderly parents with words and actions that show frustration saying that their words don't make sense?

Of course there can be times when you and your parents have conflicting opinions due to differences in generation, education, or culture. However, we should always try to respect and honor our parents' opinions first. Although we may be correct, as long as their opinions don't contradict the Bible, we should be able to yield our own opinions for theirs.

We should never forget to honor our parents by understanding that we were able to live and mature thus far because of their love and sacrifice for us. Some people may feel like their parents never did anything for them and find it hard to honor them. However, even if some parents may not have been faithful with their responsibilities as parents, we must remember that honoring the parents who gave us birth is basic human civility.

If You Love God, Honor Your Parents

Loving God and honoring your parents go hand in hand. 1 John 4:20 says, *"If someone says, 'I love God,' and hates his brother, he is a liar; for the one who does not love his brother whom he has seen, cannot love God whom he has not seen."*

If someone claims to love God but does not love his parents and does not live peacefully with his brothers and sisters, then that person is being hypocritical, and he is lying. That is why in

Matthew 15 verses 4-9 we see Jesus scolding the Pharisees and scribes. According to the traditions of the elders, as long as they were giving their offerings to God, they didn't have to worry about giving to their parents.

If someone says he cannot give anything to his parents because he has to give to God, this not only breaks God's commandment about honoring one's parents, but since he is using God as an excuse, it's clear that this is coming from an evil heart; wanting to take away what's rightfully due to his parents to satisfy himself. Someone who truly loves and honors God from the center of his heart will love and honor his parents as well.

For instance, if someone who had trouble loving his parents in the past comes to understand God's love more and more, he will begin to better understand his parents' love as well. The more you come into the truth, cast out sins, and live according to God's word, the more your heart will become filled with true love, and the more you will be able to serve and love your parents as a result.

The Blessings You Receive when You Obey the Fifth Commandment

God made a promise to those who love God and honor their parents. Exodus 20:12 says, *"Honor your father and your mother, that your days may be prolonged in the land which the LORD your God gives you."*

This verse doesn't simply mean that you will live a long life if you honor your parents. It means that as much as you honor God and honor your parents in His truth, He will respectively bless you with prosperity and protection in all areas of your life. "Living long" means that God will bless you, your family, your workplace or business from sudden disasters so that your life will be long and thriving.

Ruth, a woman from the Old Testament, received this kind of blessing. Ruth was a Gentile from the land of Moab, and looking at her physical circumstances, one would say that she was having a tough life. She married a Jewish man who had left Israel to avoid a famine. But not long after they were married, he passed away and left her without any children.

Her father-in-law had already passed away, and there was no man in the house to support the family. The only other people left in her household were her mother-in-law, Naomi, and her sister-in-law, Orpah. When her mother-in-law, Naomi decided to return to Judah, Ruth quickly decided to follow her.

Naomi tried to persuade her young daughter-in-law to leave and try to start a new, happier life, but Ruth couldn't be persuaded. Ruth wanted to care for her widowed mother-in-law to the end, so she ended up following her to Judah, a land totally foreign to her. Because she loved her mother-in-law, she wanted to fulfill all her duties as a daughter-in-law. She wanted to do her best by caring for Naomi as long as she could. To do this, she was even willing to give up the chance of finding a new, happier life for herself.

Ruth had also come to have faith in the God of Israel through her mother-in-law. We can see her touching confession in Ruth chapter 1, verses 16 through 17:

> *Do not urge me to leave you or turn back from following you; for where you go, I will go, and where you lodge, I will lodge. Your people shall be my people, and your God, my God. Where you die, I will die, and there I will be buried. Thus may the LORD do to me, and worse, if anything but death parts you and me.*

When God heard this confession, even though Ruth was a Gentile, He blessed her and made her life prosperous. According to the Jewish custom where a woman could remarry with one of her deceased husband's kinsman, Ruth was able to start a new, happy life with a kind husband and live the rest of her life with her mother-in-law, whom she loved.

On top of that, through her blood line came King David, and Ruth also had the privilege of sharing in the genealogy of the Savior Jesus Christ. As God promised, because Ruth honored her parent in God's love, she received abundant physical and spiritual blessings.

Like Ruth, we need to love God first, and then honor our parents in God's love, and thereby receive all the promised blessings that are included in God's words, "you may live long in the land."

Chapter 7
The Sixth Commandment

"You Shall Not Murder"

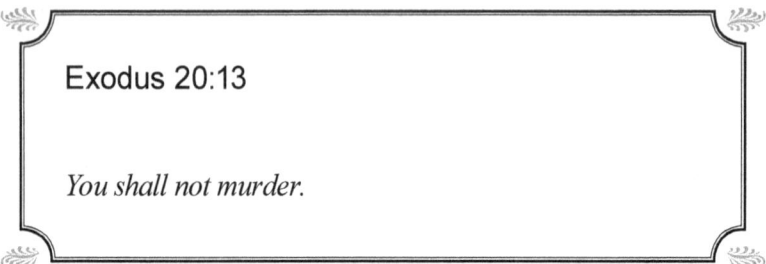

As a pastor, I get to interact with many church members. Aside from the normal worship services, I get to meet them when they come to receive prayer, share their testimony, or seek spiritual encouragement.

In order to help them grow stronger in their faith, I often ask them this question, "Do you love God?"

"Yes! I love God," most people will confidently answer. But this is often because they do not understand the true spiritual meaning of loving God. So I share with them the verse, *"For this is the love of God, that we keep His commandments"* (1 John 5:3) and explain the spiritual meaning of loving God. Then when I ask the same question again, most people answer with less confidence the second time around.

It's very important to understand the spiritual meaning of God's words. And this is the same case with the Ten Commandments. So what spiritual significance does the sixth commandment carry?

"You Shall Not Murder"

If we look at Genesis chapter four, we witness mankind's very first case of murder. This is the case where Adam's son, Cain, kills his younger brother Abel. Why do things like this happen?

Abel made a sacrifice to God in a way that pleased God.

Cain made a sacrifice to God in a way that he thought was right, and the way that was most comfortable for himself. When God did not accept Cain's sacrifice, instead of trying to figure out what he had done wrong, Cain became jealous of his brother and became filled with anger and resentment.

God knew Cain's heart, and on several occasions, He warned Cain. God told him, *"Its[sin] desire is for you, but you must master it"* (Genesis 4:7). But as it is written in Genesis 4:8, *"When they were in the field, that Cain rose up against Abel his brother and killed him,"* Cain was unable to control the anger in his heart and ended up committing the irreversible sin.

From the words "When they were in the field," we can guess that Cain was waiting for the moment when he would be alone with his brother. This means that Cain had already decided in his heart to kill his brother, and he was looking for the right chance. The murder Cain committed was not accidental; it was the result of his uncontrolled anger which turned into action at a single moment. This is what makes Cain's murder such a great sin.

Following Cain's murder, numerous other murder cases occurred throughout the history of mankind. And today, because the world is full of sins, countless murders occur every day. The average age of criminals are going down, and the types of crimes are becoming more and more evil. What's worse is that nowadays, murder cases where parents kill their children and children kill their parents are not so shocking anymore.

Physical Murder: Taking Another Person's Life

Legally, there are two types of murder: there is first degree murder, where one person kills another person intentionally for a specific reason; and then there is second degree murder, where a person unintentionally kills another person. Murder out of malice or material gain or accidental murder through reckless driving are all types of murder; however the weight of sin for each case varies, depending on the situation. Some murders are not considered sin, such as shedding blood on the battle field or killing out of legitimate self-defense.

The Bible says that if a person kills a thief that breaks into his house at night, it is not to be considered murder, but if a person kills a thief that breaks into his house in the day, it is considered excessive self-defense, and he should face punishment. This is because several thousand years ago, at the time God gave us His laws, people could easily chase out or catch a thief with the help of another person.

God considered excessive self-defense that causes the bloodshed of another a sin in this case, because God forbids the neglect of human rights and abuse of the dignity of life. This shows God's just and loving nature (Exodus 22:2-3).

Suicide and Abortion

Aside from the aforementioned types of murders, there is also the case of 'suicide.' 'Suicide' is clearly considered 'murder' before God. God has sovereignty over the lives of all people, and suicide is the act of denying this sovereignty. This is why suicide is a great sin.

But people commit this sin because they don't believe in life after death, or they don't believe in God. So on top of committing the sin of disbelief in God, they are also committing the sin of murder. So imagine what kind of judgment awaits them!

Nowadays, with the surge of Internet users, there are frequent cases where people are tempted by websites to commit suicide. In Korea, the number one cause of death among people in their forties is cancer, and the second cause is suicide. This is becoming a serious social problem. People must understand the fact that they do not have the authority to end their own lives, and that just because they have finished their life here on earth, it doesn't mean that the problem they leave behind gets resolved.

Then what about abortions? The truth of the matter is that the life of a child in the womb is under God's sovereign power, so abortion also falls under the category of murder.

Today, in a time when sin controls so many people's lives, parents abort their children without even considering it a sin. Murdering another person is in itself a terrible sin, but if parents take the life of their own child, how greater is the sin?

Physical murder is a clear sin, so every country has very strict laws against it. It is also a grave sin before God, so the enemy devil can bring all kinds of trials and tribulations to those who commit murder. Not only that, a fierce judgment awaits them in the afterlife, so no one should ever commit the sin of murder.

Spiritual Murder that Harms the Spirit and Soul

God considers physical murder a terrible sin, but He also considers spiritual murder—which is just as terrible—as a grave sin as well. Then what exactly is spiritual murder?

First, spiritual murder is when a person does something outside of God's truth, either through words or actions, and ends up making another person stumble in faith.

To make another believer stumble is to harm his spirit by making him move away from God's truth.

Let's say a young believer came up to one of the church

leaders to get counseling and he asked, "Is it okay if I miss Sunday worship to take care of some very important business?" If the leader advises him, "Well, if it's for such an important business, I guess it's okay for you to miss Sunday worship," then this leader is making the young believer stumble.

Or let's say someone in charge of the church treasury asks, "Can I borrow some of the church money for personal use? I can pay it all back in just a couple of days." If the church leader answers, "As long as you pay it back eventually, it doesn't really matter," then the leader is teaching him something that contradicts God's will, therefore he is harming his fellow believer's spirit.

Or if a small group leader says, "We're living in such a busy world these days. How can we possibly meet often?" and he teaches his fellow believers not to take church meetings seriously, he is teaching against God's truth, and so he is making his fellow believers stumble (Hebrews 10:25). As it is written, *"If a blind man guides a blind man, both will fall into a pit"* (Matthew 15:14).

So teaching other believers untruthful information and causing them to stumble away from God's truth is a type of spiritual murder. Giving believers false information can cause them to experience tribulations for no reason. That's why church leaders in the position of teaching other believers should pray fervently before God and give out correct information, or they should refer their questions to another leader who can clearly get the right answer from God and steer the growing believers in the right direction.

Furthermore, saying things one should not say, or saying evil words can fall into the category of spiritual murder. Saying things that condemn or judge others, creating a synagogue of Satan by gossiping, or creating dissension between people are all examples of provoking another person to hate or act out of evil.

What's worse is when people spread rumors about a servant of God, like pastors, or about a church. These rumors can make many people stumble, and therefore those who spread these rumors will surely face judgment before God.

In some cases, we see people harming their own spirits out of the evil in their hearts. Examples of these types of people are the Jews that tried to kill Jesus—even though He was acting in the truth—or Judas Iscariot who betrayed Jesus by selling Him over to the Jews for thirty silver coins.

If someone stumbles after seeing someone else's weaknesses, that person should know that he too, has evil in himself. There are times when people look at a newborn Christian who hasn't thrown away his former ways yet and says, "And he calls himself a Christian? I'm not going to church because of him." This is a case where they are making themselves stumble. No one else caused this upon them; rather they are harming themselves out of their own evil and judgmental heart.

In some cases, people may fall away from God after becoming disappointed with someone who they believed to be a strong Christian, claiming that he acted out of untruth. If they just focused on God and the Lord Jesus Christ, they wouldn't stumble, nor would they leave the road of salvation.

For example, there are times when people co-sign for a person they really trust and respect, but for one reason or another something goes wrong, and the co-signer faces a hardship as a result. In this case, many people become very disappointed and offended. When something like this occurs, they need to understand that the situation only proves that their faith was not true faith, and they should repent for their disobedience. They are the ones who disobeyed God when He specifically told us not to put up security for debts (Proverbs 22:26).

And if you truly have a good heart and true faith, when you see someone else's weakness, you should pray for him with a compassionate heart and wait for him to change.

In addition, some people may be a stumbling block to themselves after becoming offended while listening to God's message. If, for example, the pastor is giving a sermon on a specific sin, even though the pastor never even thought of them, let alone mentioned their name, they think, "The pastor is talking about me! How could he do that in front of all those people?" And then they leave the church.

Or when the pastor says that the tithe belongs to God and that God blesses those who tithe, some people complain that the church is putting too much emphasis on money. And then when the pastor testifies about God's power and His miracles, some people say, "That doesn't make sense to me," and complain that the messages don't sit well with their knowledge and education. These are all examples of people getting offended on their own and creating their own stumbling blocks in their hearts.

Jesus said in Matthew 11:6, *"And blessed is he who does not take offense at Me,"* and in John 11:10 He said, *"But if anyone walks in the night, he stumbles, because the light is not in him."* If someone has a good heart and desires to receive the truth, he won't stumble or fall away from God, because His word, which is the light, will be with him. If someone trips over a stumbling block or becomes offended by something, it only proves that darkness is still left in him.

Of course when one becomes easily offended, it's a sign that he is either weak in his faith or has darkness in his heart. But a person that offends another person is also responsible for his actions. For a person delivering a message to another person, even though what he is saying is the absolute truth, he should try to deliver it wisely, in a way that connects with the receiver's level of faith.

If you tell a newborn Christian who just received the Holy Spirit, "If you want to be saved, quit drinking and smoking," or "You should never open your store on Sundays," or "If you commit the sin of ceasing to pray, that becomes a wall between you and God, so make sure you come to church and pray every day," that's equivalent to feeding meat to a baby that should be nursed. Even if the newborn Christian obeys under pressure, they'll probably think, "Oh man, being a Christian is very difficult," and they may feel burdened, and sooner or later, give up their faith walk altogether.

Matthew 18:7 says, *"Woe to the world because of its stumbling blocks! For it is inevitable that stumbling blocks come; but woe to that man through whom the stumbling block comes!"* Even if you say something for the benefit of another person, if what you say causes the other person to become offended or fall away from God, that is considered spiritual murder, and you will inevitably face some trials to pay the price of this sin.

So if you love God, and if you love others, you should practice self-control with each word that you say, so that what you say brings grace and blessings to everyone who listens. Even if you are teaching someone in the truth, you should try to be sensitive and see if what you're saying is making him feel accused and heavy in the heart, or if it's giving him hope and strength to apply the teaching to his life, so that everyone you minister to can walk the glorious road of a life in Christ Jesus.

The Spiritual Murder of Hating Another Brother

The second type of spiritual murder is hating another brother or sister in Christ.

It is written in 1 John 3:15, *"Everyone who hates his brother is a murderer; and you know that no murderer has eternal life abiding in him."*

This is because basically, the root of murder is hatred. At first, someone may hate another person in his heart. But when that hate grows, it can cause him to carry out an evil act against that other person, and in the end, this hate might even cause him to commit murder. In Cain's case as well, it all began when Cain started hating his brother Abel.

This is why in Matthew 5:21-22 it says, *"You have heard that the ancients were told, 'You shall not commit murder and whoever commits murder shall be liable to the court.' But I say to you that everyone who is angry with his brother shall be guilty before the court; and whoever says to his brother, 'You good-for-nothing,' shall be guilty before the supreme court;*

and whoever says, 'You fool,' shall be guilty enough to go into the fiery hell."

When a person hates other persons in his heart, his anger may cause him to fight with them. And if something good happens to the person he hates, he may become jealous and judgmental, condemning the other person and spreading word about his weaknesses. He may deceive him and cause him harm, or become enemies with him. Hating another person and acting toward another person out of evil are examples of spiritual murder.

In the Old Testament times, because God hadn't sent the Holy Spirit yet, it was not easy for people to be circumcised in the heart and become holy. But now, in the New Testament times, since we can receive the Holy Spirit in our hearts, the Holy Spirit gives us the power to get rid of even our deepest sinful natures.

Being one of the Trinity God, the Holy Spirit is like a detail-oriented mother who teaches us about God the Father's heart. The Holy Spirit teaches us about sin, righteousness, and the judgment, thereby helping us to live in the truth. This is why we can throw away even the mere image of sin.

This is why God not only tells His children never to commit physical murder, but He also tells us to cast out even the root of hate from our hearts. Only when we can throw away all the evil from our hearts and fill it with love can we truly dwell in God's love and enjoy the evidence of His love (1 John 4:11-12).

When we love someone, we don't see his fallacies. And if that person happens to have a weakness, we will feel sympathy for him, and with a hopeful heart, encourage him and give him the power to change. When we were still sinners, God gave us this kind of love so we could receive salvation and go to heaven.

So we should not only obey His commandment, "You shall not murder," but we should also love all people—even our enemies—with the love of Christ and receive God's blessings all the time. And in the end, we will enter the most beautiful place in heaven and dwell in God's love for eternity.

Chapter 8
The Seventh Commandment

"You Shall Not Commit Adultery"

Exodus 20:14

You shall not commit adultery.

Mount Vesuvius, located in southern Italy, was an active volcano that only gave off steam once in a while and people thought it was only making a beautiful scenery of Pompeii.

On August 24, 79 A.D., around noon, as land tremors grew stronger and stronger, a mushroom cloud erupted out of Mount Vesuvius and blocked out the sky over Pompeii. With a great explosion, the top of the mountain cracked open and molten rock and ashes began raining down on the earth.

Within minutes, countless people died while survivors ran to the ocean for their lives. But then the worst thing that could possibly happen, happened. The wind suddenly took speed and blew against the ocean.

Once more, heat and toxic gas engulfed the citizens of Pompeii who had just survived the eruption by fleeing to the ocean, and suffocated them all.

Pompeii was a reveling city full of lust and idols. Its last day reminds us of the cities Sodom and Gomorrah from the Bible, that experienced God's judgment of fire. The fate of these cities is a clear reminder of how much God detests lustful hearts and idol worship. This is clearly stated in the Ten Commandments.

"You Shall Not Commit Adultery"

Adultery is the sexual interaction between a man and a woman who are not each other's spouse. A long time ago, adultery was considered an extremely immoral act. But what about today? Because of the development of computers and the Internet, adults, and even children have access to lustful material right at their fingertips.

The ethics about sex in today's society has become so dilapidated that sensual or obscene images are shown on television, movies, and even children's cartoons. And boldly exposing the body is spreading quickly in fashion trends. And as a result, the wrong understanding about sex is spreading rapidly.

To get to the truth of this matter, let's study the meaning of the seventh commandment, "You Shall Not Commit Adultery," in three parts.

Adultery in Action

The people's sense of moral values today is worse than ever before. So much so that in movies and television dramas, adultery is very often pictured as a beautiful type of love. And these days, unmarried men and women easily give their bodies to each other and even have pre-marital sex, thinking, "It's okay because we're going to be married in the future." Even married men and women openly profess that they have relationships with other people who are not their spouse. And to make matters worse, the age at which people are experiencing sexual relationships is becoming younger and younger.

If you look at the laws that existed when the Ten Commandments were given to Moses, people who committed the act of adultery were punished severely. Although God is love, adultery is an unacceptably serious sin, which is why He clearly draws the line and forbids it.

Leviticus 20:10 states, *"If there is a man who commits adultery with another man's wife, one who commits adultery with his friend's wife, the adulterer and the adulteress shall surely be put to death."* And in the New Testament times, the act of adultery is considered a sin that destroys the body and soul and denies the adulterer salvation.

> *"Or do you not know that the unrighteous will not inherit the kingdom of God? Do not be deceived; neither fornicators, nor idolaters, nor adulterers, nor effeminate, nor homosexuals, nor thieves, nor the covetous, nor drunkards, nor revilers, nor swindlers, will inherit the kingdom of God"* (1 Corinthians 6:9-10).

If a new believer commits this sin because of an ignorance of the truth, he may receive God's grace and gain an opportunity to repent for his sins. But if someone who is supposed to be a spiritually mature believer with an awareness of God's truth continues to commit this kind of sin, it's hard for him to even receive the spirit of repentance.

Leviticus 20:13-16 talks about the sin of having sexual

relations with an animal and the sin of having homosexual relations. In this day and age, there are countries that legally accept homosexual relationships; however, this is an abomination before God. Some people may respond saying, "Times have changed," but no matter how much times change, and no matter how much the world changes, God's word, which is the truth, never changes. Therefore if someone is a child of God, he should not defile himself by following the trends of this world.

Adultery in the Mind

When God talks about adultery, He's not simply talking about the act of committing adultery. The outward act of committing adultery is a clear case of adultery, but taking pleasure in imagining or watching immoral acts also fall under the category of adultery.

Lustful thoughts cause one to have a lustful heart; and this is the case of committing adultery in the heart. Even though one may not have done anything with physical actions, if, for instance, a man sees a woman and commits adultery in his heart, God, who looks at the center of people's hearts, considers that the same as committing physical adultery.

It says in Matthew 5:27-28, *"You have heard that it was said, 'You shall not commit adultery'; but I say to you that everyone who looks at a woman with lust for her has already committed adultery with her in his heart."* After a sinful thought enters a person's mind, it moves into his heart and then shows through his actions. Only after hate enters a person's heart does he or she begin to do things to bring harm to someone else. And only after wrath gets built up in a person's heart does he or she become angry and curse.

Likewise, when a person has lustful desires in his heart, it can easily progress into physical adultery. Even if it is not apparent, if someone commits adultery in his heart, he has already committed adultery, because the root of that sin is the same.

One day, during my first year of seminary school, I was very shocked after listening to a group of pastors talking. Up to that moment I had always loved and respected pastors and I treated them as I would the Lord. But at the end of a very heated discussion, they came to a conclusion that "as long as it was not deliberate, committing adultery in the heart is not a sin."

When God gave us the commandment, "You shall not commit adultery," didn't He give it to us because He knew we could abide by it? Since Jesus said, "I say to you that everyone who looks at a woman with lust for her has already committed adultery with her in his heart," we must simply cast out those lustful desires. There is nothing more to be said. Yes, it may be hard to do this with our own human strength, but with prayer and fasting, we can receive strength from God to easily cast out lust from our hearts.

Jesus wore the crown of thorns and shed His blood to wash away the sins we commit with our thoughts and minds. God sent to us the Holy Spirit so we can also cast off sinful natures in heart. Then what specifically can we do to cast out lust from our hearts?

The Phases of Casting out Lust from Our Hearts

Let's say for example that a beautiful woman or a handsome man passes by, and you think, "Wow, she's pretty," or "He's handsome," "I'd like to go out with her," or "I'd like to date him." Not many people would consider these thoughts as lustful or adulterous. However, if someone says these words and he really means it, then that is a sign of lust. In order to cast out even these hints of lust, we must go through the process of diligently fighting off this sin.

Normally, the more you try not to think about something, the more it pops up in your mind. After seeing an image of a man and a woman committing an immoral act in a movie, the image doesn't leave your head. Instead, the image keeps playing in your mind over and over again. Depending on how strong that image was impressed into your heart, the longer it tends to stay in your memory.

Then what can we do to cast out these lustful thoughts from our minds? First of all, we must make an effort to avoid games, magazines, or the like, that carry images that tempt us to have lustful thoughts. And when a lustful thought enters our mind, we should deter the direction of our thoughts. Let's say a lustful thought pops into your head. Instead of letting it progress, you should try to stop that thought immediately.

Then as you change these kinds of thoughts to ones that are good, true, and pleasing to God, and you continuously pray, asking for His help, He will definitely give you the strength to fight off these kinds of temptations. As long as you are willing and praying with passion, God's grace and power will come upon you. And with the help of the Holy Spirit, you will be able to cast out these sinful thoughts.

But the important thing to remember here is that you should not stop after one or two tries. You must continue praying with faith to the bitter end. It may take a month, a year, or even two to three years. But however long it may be, you should always trust in God and pray continually. Then God will give you the strength to one day defeat and throw out lust from your heart once and for all.

Once you pass the phase where you can "Stop Wrong Thoughts," you will then enter the phase where you can

"Control Your Heart." At this phase, even if you see a lustful image, if you decide with your heart, "I'd better not think about this," then the thought will not enter your mind again. Adultery in the heart comes through a combination of thoughts and feelings, and if you can control your thoughts, then sins that come from those thoughts won't have a chance to enter your heart.

The next phase is one where "Improper Thoughts Just Don't Occur" anymore. Even if you see a lustful image, your mind is not influenced by it, and so lust cannot enter your heart. The next phase is the phase where "You Can't Even Deliberately Have Improper Thoughts."

Once you get to this phase, even if you try to have lustful thoughts, it just doesn't happen. Because you have pulled that sin out by the roots, even if you see a lust-provoking image, you have no thoughts or feelings about it. This means that untruthful—or ungodly—images can no longer enter your mind.

Of course while going through the phases of casting out this sin, there may be times when you thought you cast everything out, but the sin creeps back to you somehow.

But if you believe in God's words, and you have a desire to obey His commands and cast out your sins, you won't be stagnant in your faith walk. It's like peeling an onion. When you peel off one or two layers, it may seem that the layers never end, but just several layers later, you realize you've peeled all the layers away.

Believers who look at themselves with faith do not grow disappointed, thinking, "I tried so hard, but I'm still not able to throw out this sinful nature." On the contrary, they should have faith that they will change to the extent they try to cast out sins. And with that in mind, they should strive even harder. If you realize you still have that sinful nature, you should rather be thankful that you now have the opportunity to get rid of it.

If, while going through the phases of casting out lust from your life, a lustful thought enters your mind for one second, do not be troubled. God will not consider that as committing adultery. If you dwell in that thought and let it progress further, then it becomes a great sin, but if you repent right away and continue in your efforts to become sanctified, God will look upon you with grace and give you the power to have victory over that sin.

Committing Spiritual Adultery

Committing adultery with the body is interpreted as committing adultery in the flesh, but something more serious than committing physical adultery is committing spiritual adultery. "Spiritual adultery" is when a person claims to be a believer and yet loves the world more than God. If you think about it, the fundamental reason that a person commits physical adultery is because he has a greater love for fleshly pleasures than the love for God in his heart.

Colossians 3:5-6 reads, *"Therefore consider the members of your earthly body as dead to immorality, impurity, passion, evil desire, and greed, which amounts to idolatry. For it is because of these things that the wrath of God will come upon the sons of disobedience."* This means that even if we receive the Holy Spirit, experience God's miracles, and have faith, if we don't cast out greed and undue desires from our hearts, then we are prone to love the things of the world more than God.

We learned from the second commandment that the spiritual interpretation of idol worship is loving something more than God. Then what is the difference between "spiritual idol worship" and "spiritual adultery"?

Idol worship is when people who don't know God create some sort of image and worship it. The spiritual interpretation of "idol worship" is when believers with weak faith love the things of the world more than God.
For some new believers whose faith is still weak, it is possible for them to love the world more than God. They may have questions like, "Does God really exist?" or "Does heaven and hell really exist?" Since they still have doubt, it's hard for them to live according to the word. They may still love money, fame,

or their family more than God, and thereby commit spiritual idol worship.

However, as they listen to the word more and more, and as they pray and experience God answering their prayers, they begin to realize that the Bible is true. And then they can believe that heaven and hell really exist. Subsequently, they come to realize the reason why they truly need to love God first and foremost. If their faith grows like this, and they still continue to love and chase after the things of the world, then they are committing "spiritual adultery."

Let's say for example, there was a man who had a simple thought, "It would be nice to marry that woman," and that woman happened to get married to some other man. In this case, we cannot say that that woman committed adultery. Since the man who had the wishful thought simply had a crush, and the woman had no relationship with this man, we cannot say she committed adultery. To be more exact, that woman was just an idol in the man's heart.

On the contrary, if the man and woman dated each other, confirmed their love for each other, and got married, and then the woman had an immoral relationship with another man, this would be considered committing adultery. So you can see that spiritual idol worship and committing spiritual adultery are seemingly alike, but they are two very different things.

The Relationship between the Israelites and God

The Bible compares the relationship between the Israelites and God to the relationship between a father and his children. This relationship is also compared to that of a husband and wife. This is because their relationship is like that of a couple who has made a covenant of love. However, if you look at the history of Israel, there are many times when the people of Israel forget about this covenant and worship foreign gods.

Gentiles worshipped idols because they didn't know God, but the Israelites, despite the fact that they knew God so well from the beginning, worshipped foreign idols out of their selfish desires.

That is why in 1 Chronicles 5:25 it says, *"But they acted treacherously against the God of their fathers and played the harlot after the gods of the peoples of the land, whom God had destroyed before them,"* meaning that the Israelites' idol worship was, in fact, spiritual adultery.

Jeremiah 3:8 reads, *"And I saw that for all the adulteries of faithless Israel, I had sent her away and given her a writ of divorce, yet her treacherous sister Judah did not fear; but she went and was a harlot also."* As a result of Solomon's sin, during his son, Rehoboam's reign, Israel split into Northern Israel and Southern Judah. Shortly after this division, Northern Israel committed spiritual adultery by worshipping idols, and as a result, were disowned and destroyed by God's wrath. Then, Southern Judah, even after seeing all this happen to Northern Israel, instead of repenting, they too continued on worshipping their idols.

All of God's children living now in the New Testament times are brides of Jesus Christ. This is why apostle Paul confessed that when it comes to meeting the Lord, he worked hard to prepare the believers to be pure brides for Christ, who is their husband (2 Corinthians 11:2).

So if a believer calls the Lord "My Groom," while he or she continues to love the world and live away from the truth, then he or she is committing spiritual adultery (James 4:4). If a husband or wife betrays his/her spouse and commits physical adultery, it is a terrible sin that is hard to forgive. If someone betrays God and the Lord and commits spiritual adultery, how much more terrible is his sin?

In Jeremiah chapter 11, we can see God telling Jeremiah not to pray for Israel, since the people of Israel refused to stop committing spiritual adultery. He even goes on to say that even if the people of Israel cry out to Him, He will not listen to them.

So if the severity of spiritual adultery reaches a certain point, the person committing it won't be able to hear the voice of the Holy Spirit; and no matter how hard he prays, his prayer will not be answered. As one grows further away from God, he becomes more worldly, and thus ends up committing severe sins that lead to death—sins such as physical adultery. As it is recorded in Hebrews chapter 6 or chapter 10, this is like crucifying Jesus Christ all over again, and thereby walking toward the way of death.

Therefore let us cast away the sins of committing adultery in the spirit, mind, and or body, and with holy conduct, meet the qualifications to become the Lord's brides—spotless and without blemish—carrying out a blessed life that brings joy to the Father's heart.

Chapter 9
The Eighth Commandment

"You Shall Not Steal"

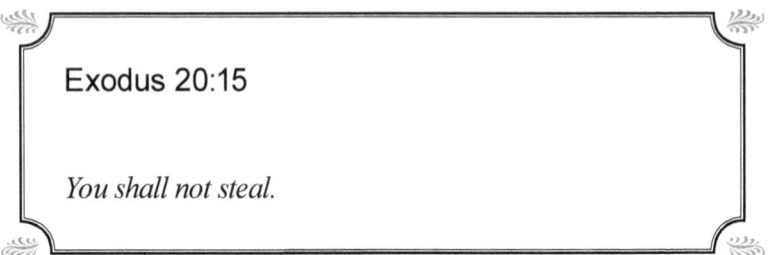

Exodus 20:15

You shall not steal.

Obedience to the Ten Commandments directly affects our salvation and our ability to overcome, conquer, and rule over the power of the enemy devil and Satan. To the Israelites, obeying or disobeying the Ten Commandments determined whether they were one of God's chosen people or not.

Likewise, for us who have become God's children, whether we obey or disobey God's words determines whether we are saved or not. This is because our obedience to God's commands creates a standard for our faith. So obedience to the Ten Commandments is tied to our salvation, and these commandments are also God's provision of love and blessings for us.

"You Shall Not Steal."

There is an old Korean saying, "A needle thief becomes a cow thief." This means that if people commit a petty crime and they go unpunished, and they keep repeating the negative action, pretty soon they may end up committing a much more serious crime with great, negative consequences. This is why God warns us, "You shall not steal."

This is an account of a man named Fu Pu-ch'i, who was styled "Tsze-tsien" or "Tzu-chien" and one of the disciples of Confucius" and commandant of Tan-fu in the state of Lu, during China's Chunqiu (Spring and Autumn) Period and Warring States Period. There was news that the soldiers of the neighboring Qi state were about to attack, and Fu Pu-ch'i ordered that the walls of the kingdom be tightly shut.

It happened to be harvest time and the crops in farmer's fields were ripe for harvest. The people asked, "Before closing up the walls can we harvest the crops in the fields, before the enemies arrive?" Disregarding the people's request, Fu Pu-ch'i had the walls closed. Then the people began resenting Fu Pu-ch'i, claiming that he was in favor of the enemies, and so he was summoned to the king for an inquiry. When the king questioned him about his actions, Fu Pu-ch'i answered, "Yes, it's a great loss for us if our enemies took all of our crops, but if our people, in haste, get into the habit of collecting crops from fields that don't belong to them, it will be hard to break them from this habit even after ten years." With this statement, Fu Pu-ch'i earned great respect and admiration from the king.

Fu Pu-ch'i could have let the people collect the crops as they requested, but if they learn to somehow justify their action of stealing from someone else's field, then the lasting consequences could be more detrimental to the people and their kingdom in the long run. So "stealing" means handling something in a wrong way with a wrong motivation; or taking something not belonging to oneself, or furtively possessing someone else's property.

But the "stealing" that God talks about also has a deeper and wider spiritual interpretation as well. So what is incorporated in the meaning of "stealing," in the eighth commandment?

Taking Someone Else's Belongings: the Physical Definition of Stealing

The Bible specifically forbids stealing, and it outlines specific rules about what should be done when someone steals (Exodus 22).

If a stolen animal is found alive in the thief's possession, the thief must pay back to the owner double the amount that he stole. If a man steals an animal and slaughters it or sells it, he must pay back to the owner five times the portion for oxen and four for sheep. No matter how small an item is, taking someone else's belonging is stealing, which even society labels as a crime and for which there are specific punishments.

Aside from the obvious cases of stealing, there are cases where people could steal by being neglectful. For example, in our everyday life, we may be in the habit of using other people's things without asking and without much thought. We may not even feel guilty about using it without permission, because maybe we're either close to that person or the item we're using is not very valuable.

It's the same case when we use our spouse's things without permission. Even in an inevitable situation, if we use someone's things without permission, as soon as we're done using it, we should return it right away. However, there are many times when we don't even return it at all.

This is not only causing someone a loss; it's an act of disrespect towards that person. Even though it may not be considered a serious crime according to society's laws, this is considered stealing in God's eyes. If they have a really clean conscience, and they take something—no matter how small or invaluable—from someone without permission, they will feel guilty about it.

Even if we don't steal or take something by force, if we acquire someone else's belongings in an improper way, it's still considered stealing. Using one's position or power to receive a bribe would also fall into this category. Exodus 23:8 warns, *"You shall not take a bribe, for a bribe blinds the clear-sighted and subverts the cause of the just."*

Vendors with a good heart will feel guilty when they overprice their customers to extort more profit for themselves. Even though they didn't steal someone else's possession in secret, this act is still considered stealing because they took more than their fair share.

Spiritual Stealing: Taking what Belongs to God

Aside from the "stealing" where you take from another person without permission, there is "spiritual stealing" where you take from God without permission. This can actually affect one's salvation.

Judas Iscariot, one of Jesus' disciples, was in charge of managing all the offerings that people gave after being healed and or being blessed by Jesus. But with the passage of time, greed entered into his heart, and he began to steal (John 12:6).

In John chapter 12, where Jesus visits Simon's house in Bethany, we encounter a scene where a woman comes and pours perfume on Jesus. Upon seeing this, Judas chastises her, asking why the perfume wasn't sold and the money given to the poor. If the expensive perfume had been sold, then he, as the keeper of the money bag, could have helped himself to that money, but since it was poured on Jesus' feet, he felt like that was a profitable item gone to waste.

Ultimately, Judas, who became a slave to money, sold Jesus over for thirty silver coins. Although he had the opportunity to receive the glory of being called one of Jesus' disciples, he instead stole from God and sold his teacher, piling up his sins. Unfortunately, he couldn't even receive the spirit of repentance before he took his own life and met his miserable end (Acts 1:18).

This is why we need to take a closer look at what happens if one steals from God.

The First Case Is if Someone Puts His Hand on the Church Treasury.

Even if the thief happens to be a non-believer, if he steals from the church, he is bound to feel some sort of fear in his heart. But if a believer puts his hand on God's money, how can he say he even has the faith to receive salvation?

Even if people never find out, God sees everything, and when the time comes, He will conduct His judgment of justice, and the thief will have to pay the penalty of his sin. If the thief isn't able to repent of his sins and dies without receiving salvation, how terrible would that be? By that time, no matter how much he beats his chest and regrets for his actions, it would be too late. He shouldn't have touched God's money from the very beginning.

The Second Case Is if Someone Abuses the Church's Belongings or Misuses the Church Money.

Even if one may not have stolen offerings directly, if he uses money collected for some membership fees of mission groups or other donations for their personal use, that is the same thing as stealing from God. It's also stealing if one buys office supplies or stationary with the church money and uses it for his personal needs.

Wasting church supplies, taking out church funds to purchase supplies and using the leftover change for other purposes instead of returning it back to the church, or using the church phone, electricity, equipment, furniture, or other supplies for personal use without discretion are also forms of mishandling the church money.

We must also make sure children do not fold or tear offering envelopes, church bulletins or newspapers for fun or play. Some may think these are petty or insignificant misdemeanors, but on a spiritual level, it's basically stealing from God, and these actions may become barriers of sin between us and God.

The Third Case Is Stealing Tithes and Offerings.

In Malachi 3:8-9, it says, *"Will a man rob God? Yet you are robbing Me! But you say, 'How have we robbed You?' In tithes and offerings. You are cursed with a curse, for you are robbing Me, the whole nation of you!"*

Tithing is giving God a tenth of our earnings, as proof that we understand that He is the Master over all material things and that He oversees all of our lives. That is why if we say we believe in God and yet do not make our tithes, we are stealing from God, and then a curse can creep into our lives. This doesn't mean God will curse us. It means that when Satan accuses us of this wrongdoing, God cannot protect us, because in actuality, we are breaking God's spiritual law. Therefore we may experience financial problems, temptations, sudden disasters or illnesses.

But as it says in Malachi 3:10, *"'Bring the whole tithe into the storehouse, so that there may be food in My house, and test Me now in this,' says the LORD of hosts, 'if I will not open for you the windows of heaven and pour out for you a blessing until it overflows.'"* When we give proper tithes, we can receive God's promised blessings and protection.

Then there are some people who don't receive God's protection because they don't give their whole tithes. Without taking into account other sources of income, people calculate their tithes on their net salary, instead of their gross salary, and that's after subtracting all deductions and taxes.

But proper tithing is giving God a tenth of our total income. Income from a side business, monetary gifts, dinner invitations, or gifts are all personal profits, so we should calculate one-tenth of the value from these types of earnings and make the proper tithes for them as well.

In some cases, people calculate their tithes but offer it up to God as a different type of offering, such as missionary offerings, or good-will offerings. But this is still considered stealing from

God, because this is not a proper tithe. How the church uses the offerings is up to the church finance department, but it's up to us to give our tithes under the correct offering title.

We can also give other offerings as thanksgiving offerings. Children of God have so much to be thankful for. With the gift of salvation we can go to heaven, with different duties in the church we can reap rewards in heaven, and while living here on earth, we receive God's protection and blessing at all times, so how thankful we should be!

That's why every Sunday we come before God with various thanksgiving offerings thanking God for protecting us for another week. And on biblical festivities or occasions when we have a special reason to thank God for, we set aside a special offering and offer it up to God.

In our relationship with other people, when someone helps us or serves us in a special way, we don't merely feel thankful in our hearts; we want to give something to him in return. In the same way, it's only natural that we would want to offer something up to God to show our appreciation for giving us salvation and preparing heaven for us (Matthew 6:21).

If people say they have faith and yet are stingy about giving to God, that means that they still have greed for material things. This shows that they love material things more than God. That is why Matthew 6:24 says, *"No one can serve two* masters; for either he will hate the one and love the other, or he will be devoted to one and despise the other. You cannot serve God and wealth."

If we are mature Christians, and yet love material possessions more than God, then it's much easier for us to backslide in our faith than to move forward. The grace that we once received becomes a long-gone memory, reasons to be thankful shrink, and before we know it, our faith shrivels to the point where our salvation is in jeopardy.

God is pleased with the aroma of an offering of true thanksgiving and faith. Everyone has a different measure of faith, and God knows each person's situation, and He sees each person's inner heart. So it's not the size or amount of the offering that matters to Him. Remember that Jesus complimented the widow who offered two very small copper coins which were all she had to live on (Luke 21:2-4).

When we please God like this, God will bless us with so many blessings and reasons to be thankful that the offerings we give are incomparable to the blessings we receive from Him. God makes sure our soul is prosperous, and He blesses us so that our lives overflow with even more reasons to be thankful. God blesses us thirtyfold, sixtyfold, and one hundredfold of the offerings we lift up to Him.

After accepting Christ, as soon as I learned that we should give proper tithes and offerings to God, I began to obey immediately. I had accrued a lot of debt during the seven years that I was bedridden with illness, but because I was so thankful that God healed me of my infirmities, I always offered to God as much as I could. Even though my wife and I both worked, we were barely paying off the interest on our debt. Nevertheless, we never went to worship empty-handed.

When we believed in the omnipotent God and obeyed His words, He helped us pay off our overwhelming debt in just a few months. And in time, we were able to experience God pouring unending blessings upon us so we could live in plentitude.

The Fourth Case Is Stealing God's Words.

Stealing God's words means making a false prophecy in God's name (Jeremiah 23:30-32). For example, there are people who steal His words by saying that they heard the voice of God and they talk about the future like a fortune teller or tell a person who keeps failing in his business that "God made you fail in your business because you are supposed to become a pastor, instead of running a business."

It's also considered stealing God's word when someone has a dream or vision derived from his own thoughts and he says, "God gave me this dream," or "God gave me this vision." This also falls into the category of misusing God's name.

Of course understanding the will of God through the work of the Holy Spirit and proclaiming God's will is good, but in order to do this correctly, we need to check if we are acceptable before God. This is because God will not speak to just anyone. He can only speak to those who lack evil in their hearts. This is why we need to make sure that we are not in the slightest way stealing God's words while being immersed in our own thoughts.

Other than this, if we ever feel pangs of conscience, shame, or embarrassment when we take something or do something, this is a sign that we should reevaluate ourselves. The reason why we feel pangs of our conscience is because we might be taking something that doesn't belong to us for our own selfish motives, and the Holy Spirit inside of us is grieving.

For example, even if we don't steal some object, if we receive a wage after working lazily or if we receive a duty or a task at church but we don't fulfill our responsibilities, assuming that we have a good heart, we should feel pangs of conscience.

Also, if a person dedicated to God wastes time that is set aside for God and causes a loss of time to God's kingdom, he is stealing time. Not only with God, but also in work or informal settings, we need to make sure that we are punctual so we don't cause a loss to others by wasting their time.

Therefore we should always evaluate ourselves to make sure

we are not committing the sin of stealing in any way, and throw away selfishness and greed from our mind and hearts. And with a clean conscience, we should strive to achieve a true and sincere heart before God.

Chapter 10
The Ninth Commandment

"You Shall Not Bear False Witness against Your Neighbor"

Exodus 20:16

You shall not bear false witness against your neighbor.

It was the night Jesus was arrested. While Peter was sitting out in the courtyard where Jesus was questioned, a servant girl said to him, "You too were with Jesus the Galilean." At this, a surprised Peter retorted, "I don't know what you're talking about" (Matthew 26).

Peter did not truly deny Jesus from the bottom of his heart—he was lying because of a sudden surge of fear. Right after this incident, Peter went outside and banged his head on the ground, weeping bitterly. Then when Jesus carried the cross up to Golgotha, Peter could only follow from afar, ashamed and unable to even lift up his head.

Although all this happened before Peter received the Holy Spirit, because of this lie, he couldn't dare to be crucified like Jesus, in a standing position. Even after receiving the Holy Spirit and dedicating his whole life to His ministry, he was so ashamed of the time he had denied Jesus, and finally he volunteered to be crucified upside down.

"You Shall Not Bear False Witness against Your Neighbor"

Of the words that people speak on a daily basis, there are some words that are very important, while other words are insignificant. Some words are meaningless, and some words are evil words that either hurt or deceive other people.

Lies are evil words that deviate from the truth. Although they do not admit it, many people tell countless lies every day—both big and small. Some people proudly say, "I don't tell lies," but before they know it, they're unwittingly standing atop a mountain of lies.

Dirt, filth, and disorder can stay hidden in the dark. However, if a bright light shines into a room, even the smallest speck of dust or spot of stain stands out clearly. Likewise, God, who is the truth itself, is like the light; and He sees many people telling lies all the time.

This is why in the ninth commandment, God tells us not to give false testimony against our neighbor. Here, "neighbor" signifies parents, brothers, children—anyone other than oneself. Let's examine how God defines "false testimony" in three parts.

First, "Giving a False Testimony" Means Talking about Your Neighbor in an Untruthful Way.

We can see how terrible giving false testimony could be, for instance, when we observe trials in court. Because the testimony of a witness directly affects the final judgment, just the slightest tip of the hat could cause a great misfortune to an innocent person, and the situation can become a matter of life or death for him.

In order to prevent abuse of the witness stand or ill-practice of false testimonies, God commanded that judges listen to many different witnesses in order to correctly understand all aspects of the case so they can make wise and discreet judgments. This is why He ordered those who testify and those who judge to do so with prudence and caution.

In Deuteronomy 19:15, God says, *"A single witness shall not rise up against a man on account of any iniquity or any sin which he has committed; on the evidence of two or three witnesses a matter shall be confirmed."* He goes on to say in verse 16-20 that *"If the witness proves to be a liar, giving false testimony against his brother,"* then he should receive the punishment he intended to put upon his fellow brother.

Aside from serious cases like this one where one person causes a great loss to another person, there are so many other cases where people tell small lies here and there about their neighbors in day to day life. Even if one doesn't lie about his neighbor, if he doesn't reveal the truth in a situation where he should speak out the truth in defense of his neighbor, this can also be considered as giving false testimony.

If another person was receiving the blame for a wrong that we committed, and we don't speak up out of fear of getting into trouble ourselves, then how can we have a clean conscience? Yes, God is commanding us not to lie, but He is also commanding us to have honest hearts so that our words and actions reflect integrity and truth as well.

Then what does God think about "little white lies" that we tell to comfort someone or make someone feel better?

For example, we may be visiting a friend, and he asks us, "Did you eat?" And even though we didn't eat, we reply, "Yes, I did," so as not to bother him. However, in this case, we should still tell the truth by saying, "No, I didn't eat, but I do not want to eat right now."

There are examples of "little white lies" even in the Bible.

In Exodus chapter 1, there is a scene where the king of Egypt feels nervous because the sons of Israel have grown in great number, and he brings down a specific order on the Hebrew midwives. He tells them, *"When you are helping the Hebrew women to give birth and see them upon the birthstool, if it is a son, then you shall put him to death; but if it is a daughter, then she shall live"* (v. 16).

But the God-fearing Hebrew midwives didn't listen to the king of Egypt and kept the male babies alive. When the king summoned the midwives and asked, "Why have you done this thing, and let the boys live?" They answered, "Because the Hebrew women are not as the Egyptian women; for they are vigorous and give birth before the midwife can get to them."

Also, when Israel's first king, King Saul, became jealous of

David and tried to kill him because he was more loved by the people than himself, Jonathan, Saul's son, tricked him in order to save David's life.

In this case, where people tell a lie solely for another person's benefit, truly out of good will, and not for their own selfish motives, God will not automatically chastise them and say, "You lied." Just like He did with the Hebrew midwives, He will show His grace to them, because they were trying to save lives out of good intentions. However, when people reach a level of complete goodness, they will be able to touch the heart of the adversary or the person they are dealing without having to tell a "little white lie."

Secondly, Adding or Subtracting Words when Passing on a Message Is Another Form of Giving False Testimony.

This is the case when you relay a message about someone in a way that distorts the truth—maybe because you added your own thoughts or feelings, or omitted certain words. When someone tells them something, most people listen with subjective ears, so how they perceive the information depending heavily on their own emotions and past experiences. That's why when certain information is passed around from this person to that person, the original speaker's intended message can easily get lost.

But even if every single word—punctuation and all—is passed on accurately, depending on the messengers' intonation or emphasis on certain words, the meaning will inevitably change. For example, there is a big difference between someone lovingly asking his friend, "Why?" and someone with a cruel expression on his face shouting at his enemy, "Why?!"

That is why whenever we listen to someone, we must try to understand what he is saying without attaching any personal feelings to his message. The same rule applies when we speak to others. We should try our very best to accurately relay the original speaker's message—his intended meaning and all.

Furthermore, if the content of the message is untruthful or not necessarily helpful to the listener, even if we can accurately relay the message, it's better if we don't pass on the message at all. This is because even though we pass it on with good intentions, the receiving party may be hurt or offended; and if this happens, then we may end up stirring up discord between people.

Matthew 12:36-37 reads, *"But I tell you that every careless word that people speak, they shall give an accounting for it in the day of judgment. For by your words you will be justified, and by your words you will be condemned."* Therefore we should refrain from speaking words that are not of the truth or love in the Lord. This applies to how we should listen to words as well.

Thirdly, Judging and Criticizing Others without Really Understanding Their Heart Is also a Form of Giving False Testimony against a Neighbor.

Quite frequently, people make a judgment call about someone's heart or intentions just by looking at his expressions or actions, using their own thoughts and feelings as a guide. They may say, "That person probably said that with this in mind," or they may say, "He definitely had these intentions for acting that way."

Suppose a young worker wasn't acting too amiably with his supervisor because he was nervous about his new environment. The supervisor could think, "That new guy looks uncomfortable with me. Maybe it's because I gave him some negative critiques the other day." This is a misconception formed by the supervisor based on his own notions. In another case, someone with poor eyesight or in deep thought walks by his friend not realizing the friend was there. The friend could think, "He acts like he doesn't even know me! I wonder if he's mad at me."

And if someone else was in this same exact situation, he may show yet another reaction. Everyone has different thoughts and feelings, and so each person reacts differently to certain circumstances. Therefore, provided that everyone was given the same hardship, every individual will have a different level of strength to overcome it. This is why when we see someone in pain, we should never judge him by our own standard of tolerance for pain and think, "Why is he making such a big fuss about nothing?" It's not easy to completely understand another person's heart—even if you really love him and have a close relationship with him.

Furthermore, there are so many other ways people misjudge and misconceive others, become disappointed with them, and then finally condemn them…all because they judged others according to their own standards. If, based on our own standards we judge another person, thinking he has a specific intention in his heart even though he really doesn't, and then talk negatively about him, we are giving false testimony about him. And if we partake in this kind of act by listening to this untruth and contributing to the judging and condemning of a particular person, then once again, we are committing the sin of giving false testimony against our neighbor.

Most people think that if they themselves reacted to some situation in an evil way, then others in the same situation will do the same. Because they have a cheating heart, they think others have cheating hearts too. If they see a certain situation or scene and think evil thoughts, they think, "I bet that person is having evil thoughts too." And because they themselves look down on others, they think, "That person is looking down on me. He is conceited."

That is why it says in James 4:11, *"Do not speak against one another, brethren. He who speaks against a brother or judges his brother, speaks against the law and judges the law; but if you judge the law, you are not a doer of the law but a judge of it."* If someone judges or slanders a fellow brother, this means that he is proud, and that he ultimately wants to be like God the Judge.

And it's important to know that if we talk about other people's weakness and judge them, we are committing a sin that is much more evil.

Matthew 7:1-5 reads, *"Do not judge so that you will not be judged. For in the way you judge, you will be judged; and by your standard of measure, it will be measured to you. Why do you look at the speck that is in your brother's eye, but do not notice the log that is in your own eye? Or how can you say to your brother, 'Let me take the speck out of your eye,' and behold, the log is in your own eye? You hypocrite, first take the log out of your own eye, and then you will see clearly to take the speck out of your brother's eye."*

One more thing we have to be very careful about is judging God's words based on our own thoughts. What is impossible with man is possible with God, so when it comes to God's words, we should never say, "That's wrong."

Lying by Exaggerating or Understating the Truth

Without any evil intentions, people tend to exaggerate or understate the truth on a daily basis. For example, if someone ate a lot of food, we might say, "He ate up *everything.*" And when there's still a little bit of food left, we might say, "There is not a crumb left!" There are even times when after seeing just three or four people agree on something, we say, "*Everyone* agreed on it."

Like so, what many people don't consider a lie, is actually a lie. There are even cases where we talk about a situation of which we don't really know all the facts, and as a result, we tell a lie.

For example, let's say someone asks us how many employees work for a certain company, and we answer, "There are this many people," and then later we count and realize that the actual number is different. Even though we didn't lie intentionally, what we said is still a lie, because it is different from the truth. So in this case, a better way to answer the question would be, "I don't know the exact number, but I think there are about this many people."

Of course in these kinds of cases we weren't intentionally trying to lie with evil motives, or judging others with evil hearts. However, if we see even the slightest hint of these kinds of thoughts and actions, then it's a good idea to get to the bottom of the problem. A person whose heart is filled with the truth will not add or subtract from the truth, no matter how small the matter.

A very true and honest person can receive the truth as truth, and relay the truth as truth. So even if something is very small and unimportant, if we see ourselves talking about it with even the slightest inkling of untruth, then we should know that this signifies that our heart is not completely filled with the truth yet. And if our heart is not completely filled with the truth, this means that when put under a life-threatening situation, we are fully capable of bringing harm against another person by lying about them.

As it is written in 1 Peter 4:11, *"Whoever speaks, is to do so as one who is speaking the utterances of God,"* we should try not to lie or joke around using untruthful words. No matter what we say, we should always speak truthfully, as though we are speaking God's very words. And we can do this by praying fervently and receiving the guidance of the Holy Spirit.

Chapter 11
The Tenth Commandment

"You Shall Not Covet Your Neighbor's House"

Exodus 20:17

You shall not covet your neighbor's house; you shall not covet your neighbor's wife or his male servant or his female servant or his ox or his donkey or anything that belongs to your neighbor.

Do you know the story of the goose that laid the golden eggs, one of Aesop's famous tales? Once upon a time, in a small village lived a farmer who came to possess a strange goose. While thinking about what to do with the goose, a very shocking thing happened.

The goose began laying a golden egg every morning. And then one day, the farmer thought, "There's probably a whole lot of eggs inside that goose." And suddenly, the farmer became selfish and wanted a whole load of gold so he could become rich immediately, instead of having to wait every day to receive a single golden egg.

And when his greed became too great, the farmer cut open the goose, only to find out that there was not a speck of gold inside the goose. At that moment, the farmer realized he was wrong and regretted his actions, but it was too late.

Like this, a person's greed has no bounds. No matter how many rivers flow into the ocean, the ocean cannot be filled. Such is man's greed. No matter how much one possesses, there is no complete satisfaction. We see it every day. When people's greed becomes so great, not only do they feel unsatisfied with what they have, but they also become covetous and try to possess what others have, even if it means using ill methods. Then they end up committing a grave sin.

"You Shall Not Covet Your Neighbor's House"

To "covet" something means wanting something that doesn't belong to oneself and then trying to possess someone else's belongings using improper ways; or having a heart that desires all the fleshly things of the world.

Most crimes start with a covetous heart. Covetousness can cause people to lie, steal, rob, cheat, embezzle, murder, and commit all kinds of other crimes. There are also cases where people not only covet material things, but also position and fame as well.

Because of these covetous hearts, at times sibling relationships, parent-child relationships, even husband-wife relationships turn hostile. Some families become enemies, and instead of living happy lives in the truth, people become jealous and envious of those who have more than they do.

This is why through the tenth commandment, God warns us against covetousness, which gives birth to sin. Furthermore, God wants us to set our minds on the things above (Colossians 3:2). Only when we seek eternal life and fill our hearts with the hope of heaven can we find true satisfaction and happiness. Only then can we cast out covetousness. Luke 12:15 says, *"Beware, and be on your guard against every form of greed; for not even when one has an abundance does his life consist of his possessions."* As Jesus says, only when we cast out all covetousness can we stay away from sinning and therefore have eternal life.

The Process by which Coveting Comes out in the Form of Sin

So how does coveting turn into a sinful action? Let's say you visited an extremely wealthy home. The house is made of marble and it is absolutely enormous. The house is also filled with all kinds of luxurious things. It's enough to make someone say, "This house is marvelous. It is absolutely beautiful!"

But many people don't just stop after making this kind of comment. They go on to think, "I wish I had a house like that. I wish I could be as rich as that person…" Of course true believers won't allow this thought to develop into a thought about stealing. But through this kind of thought, "I wish I could have that too," greed can enter their heart.

And if greed enters the heart, it's only a matter of time that one commits a sin. It says in James 1:15, *"Then when lust has conceived, it gives birth to sin; and when sin is accomplished, it brings forth death."* There are some believers who, overcome by this desire or greed, end up committing a crime.

In Joshua chapter 7, we read about Achan, who is overcome by this type of greed and ends up dying as punishment. Joshua, as the leader in place of Moses, was in the process of conquering the land of Canaan. The Israelites had just laid siege upon Jericho. Joshua warned his people that everything that comes out of Jericho is devoted to God, so no one should put their hands on them.

However, upon seeing an expensive robe and some silver and gold, Achan coveted them and quietly hid them for himself. Since Joshua didn't know about this, he continued on to the next city to conquer, which was the city of Ai. Since Ai was a small city, the Israelites saw it as an easy battle. But much to their befuddlement, they lost. Then God told Joshua it was because of Achan's sin. As a result, not only Achan, but his whole family—even his livestock—had to die.

In 2 Kings, chapter five, we can read about Gehazi, the servant of Elisha, who also got leprosy because he coveted things he shouldn't have. As Elisha told him to, General Naaman washed himself seven times in the Jordan River to be cleaned of his leprosy. After being cured, he wanted to give Elisha some gifts as a token of appreciation. But Elisha refused to receive anything.

Then, as General Naaman was on his way back to his homeland, Gehazi ran after him, acting as if Elisha had sent him, and asked for some goods. He took the goods and hid them. On top of that, he returned to Elisha and tried to deceive him, despite the fact that Elisha knew what he was up to from the very beginning. And so Gehazi got the leprosy that Naaman had.

It was the same case with Ananias and his wife Sapphira from Acts chapter five. They sold a piece of their property and promised to offer to God the money they got from it. But once they had the money in their hands, their hearts changed, and they hid a portion of the money for themselves and brought the rest to the apostles. Coveting the money, they tried to deceive the apostles. But deceiving the apostles is the same as deceiving the Holy Spirit, so instantly, their souls left them, and they both died on the very spot.

Coveting Hearts Lead to Death

Coveting is a great sin that ultimately leads to death. Therefore it is vital for us to cast out covetousness from our hearts, as well as temptations and greed that make us want the fleshly things of this world. What good is it if you gain everything you want in the whole world but lose your life?

On the contrary, although you may not have all the riches in this world, if you believe in the Lord and have true life, then you are a truly rich person. As we learn from the parable of the rich man and Lazarus the beggar in Luke, chapter 16, a true blessing is receiving salvation after casting out a coveting heart.

The rich man who had no faith in God and no hope of heaven lived a splendid life—wearing fine clothing, satisfying his worldly greed, and taking pleasure in merrymaking. On the other hand, the beggar Lazarus lay begging by the rich man's gate. His life was very lowly; even the dogs came to lick the sores on his body. However, in the very center of his heart, he praised God and always had the hope of heaven.

Finally, both the rich man and Lazarus died. The beggar Lazarus was taken by angels to Abraham's side, but the rich man went to the Grave, where he was in torment. Because he was so thirsty from the agony and fires, the rich man wished for just one drop of water, but even that wish couldn't be granted.

Suppose the rich man got a second chance to live here on earth? He probably would have chosen to receive eternal life in heaven, even if that meant living a poor life here. And for someone living a very needy life here, like Lazarus, if he just learns how to fear God and lives in His light, he can also receive the blessings of material wealth while living here on earth.

After his wife Sarah died, Abraham, the father of faith, wanted to buy the cave of Machpelah to bury his wife there. The owner of the cave told him to take it for free, but Abraham refused to take it for free, and paid the full price for it. He did this because he didn't have even a trace of covetousness in his heart. If it didn't belong to him, he didn't even think about possessing it (Genesis 23:9-19).

Furthermore, Abraham loved God and obeyed His word; living a life of honesty and integrity. This is why during his life here on earth, Abraham received not only the blessings of material wealth, but also the blessings of long life, fame, power, descendants, and more. He even received the spiritual blessing of being called a 'friend of God'.

Spiritual Blessings Surpass All Material Blessings

Sometimes people ask curiously, "That person looks like such a good believer. How come it doesn't look like he's receiving many blessings?" If that person was a true follower of Christ living day to day with true faith, we would see God blessing him with the best things.

As it is written in 3 John 1:2, *"Beloved, I pray that in all respects you may prosper and be in good health, just as your soul prospers,"* God blesses us so that our soul is well, before anything else. If we live like God's holy children, throwing out all evil from our hearts and obeying His commandments, God will surely bless us so that all will be well with us, including our health.

But if someone—whose soul is not prosperous—looks like he is receiving a lot of material blessings, we cannot say it's a blessing from God. In that case, his riches can actually cause him to become greedy. His greed may give birth to sin, and in turn, he may eventually fall away from God.

When situations are hard, people may depend on God

with a clean heart and serve Him diligently with love. But too often, after receiving the material blessings in their business or workplace, their hearts begin desiring more things of the world and they begin making excuses about being too busy, and they end up growing distant from God. When their profits or earnings are low, they tend to give their tithes wholeheartedly out of thanksgiving, but when their earnings increase, and their tithes also need to increase, it's easy for their hearts to become shaken. If our hearts change like this, and we grow distant from God's words and ultimately become just like the people of the secular world, then the blessings we received could actually end up being our misfortune.

However, those whose soul is prosperous will not covet the things of the world, and even if they receive blessings of honor and fortune from God, they won't become greedy for more. And they won't grumble or complain just because they don't have good things of this world; because they would be willing to offer up everything they have—even their life—for God.

People whose souls are well, will guard their faith and serve God no matter what circumstances they are in, using the blessings they receive from God only for His kingdom and glory. And because people with a prosperous soul don't have the slightest tendency to chase after worldly pleasures, or wander in search of merriment, or walk toward the way of death, God will bless them abundantly, and even more.

This is why spiritual blessings are far more important than the physical blessings of this world that fade away like the fog. And so, above all else, we must receive spiritual blessings first.

We Should Never Seek God's Blessings to Gratify Worldly Desires

Even if we didn't yet receive the spiritual blessings of our soul being prosperous, if we continue to walk in the way of righteousness and seek God with faith, He will fill us up when the time is right. People pray for something to happen right away; however, there is a time and duration for everything under heaven, and God knows the best time. There are times when God makes us wait so that He can give us even greater blessings.

If we are asking God for something out of true faith, then we will receive the power to pray continually until we receive an answer. But if we are asking God for something out of fleshly desires, then no matter how much we pray, we won't receive the faith to truly believe, and we won't receive an answer from Him.

James 4:2-3 says, *"You do not have because you do not ask. You ask and do not receive, because you ask with wrong motives, so that you may spend it on your pleasures."* God cannot answer us when we ask for something to please our worldly desires. If a young student asks his parents for money to buy things he shouldn't buy, then the parents should not give him the money.

That is why we should not pray and seek with our own thoughts, but rather, with the power of the Holy Spirit, we should seek for things in line with God's will (Jude 1:20). The Holy Spirit knows God's heart, and He can understand the deep things of God; therefore, if you depend on the guidance of the Holy Spirit during prayer, you can quickly receive God's answer to your every prayer.

So how do we depend on the Holy Spirit's guidance and pray according to God's will?

First, we have to arm ourselves with the word of God, and apply His word to our lives, so our hearts can be like that of Christ Jesus. If we have a heart like Christ, then naturally we will pray according to God's will, and we can quickly receive an answer to all of our prayers. This is because the Holy Spirit, who knows God's heart, will watch over our hearts so we can ask for the things that we truly need.

Just like it says in Matthew 6:33, *"But seek first His kingdom and His righteousness, and all these things will be added to you,"* seek God and His kingdom first, and then ask for what you need. If you pray seeking after God's will first, you will experience God pouring down His blessings upon your life so that your cup overflows with everything you need here on earth, and even more.

This is why we should continuously lift up true and wholehearted prayers to God. When you store up powerful prayers with the guidance of the Holy Spirit on a daily basis, any covetousness or sinful natures will be cast out of your heart for good, and you will receive whatever you ask for in prayer.

The apostle Paul was a citizen of Roman Empire and studied under Gamaliel, the best and most well-known scholar of his time. However, Paul wasn't interested in the things of this world. For Christ's sake, he considered everything he had as rubbish. Like Paul, the things we most definitely need to love and desire are the teachings of Jesus Christ, or the words of truth.

If we gain all of the world's wealth, honor, power, etc., and we don't have eternal life, what good are these things? But if, like the apostle Paul, we forsake all the riches of this world and live a life according to God's will, then God will surely bless us so that our soul will prosper. And then we will be called "great" in heaven, and become successful in all areas of our lives here on earth as well.

So I pray that you can cast out any greed or covetousness from your heart and life, while diligently seeking for satisfaction with what you already have, as you keep your hope in heaven. Then I know you will always lead a life overflowing with thanksgiving and joy.

Chapter 12

The Law of Abiding with God

Proverbs 8:17

I love those who love me; and those who diligently seek me will find me.

In Matthew chapter 22, there is a scene where one of the Pharisees asks Jesus which is the greatest commandment in the law.

Jesus replied, *"'You shall love the Lord your God with all your heart, and with all your soul, and with all your mind.' This is the great and foremost commandment. The second is like it, 'You shall love your neighbor as yourself.' On these two commandments depend the whole Law and the Prophets"* (Matthew 22:37-40).

This means that if we love God with all our heart and with all our soul and with all our mind and we love our neighbors as ourselves, then we can easily obey all the other commandments as well.

If we truly love God, how could we commit sins that God detests? And if we love our neighbors as ourselves, how can we act out of evil against them?

Why God Gave Us His Commandments

So, why did God go through the trouble of giving us each and every one of the Ten Commandments, instead of just telling us, "Love your God and love your neighbor as yourself"?

This is because in the Old Testament times, before the era of the Holy Spirit, it was difficult for people to truly love from their hearts out of their own will. So through the Ten Commandments, which gave the Israelites just enough enforcement to obey Him, God led them to love and fear Him, as well as love their neighbors through their actions.

So far, we took a close look at each commandment by itself, but now let's look at the commandments as two big groups: love for God, and love for our neighbors.

Commandments 1 through 4 can be summarized as, "Love the Lord your God with all your heart and with all your soul and with all your mind." Serving only the Creator God, not making false idols or worshipping them, being careful not to misuse God's name, and keeping the Sabbath day holy are all ways of loving God.

Commandments 5 through 10 can be summarized as "Love your neighbor as yourself." Honoring one's parents, warning against murder, stealing, making false testimony, coveting, etc., are all ways of preventing evil actions against others, or our neighbors. If we love our neighbors as ourselves, we wouldn't want them to go through pain, so we should be able to obey these commandments.

We Must Love God from the Center of Our Hearts

God doesn't force us to obey His commandments. He leads

us to obey them out of our own love for Him.

It is written in Romans 5:8, *"But God demonstrates His own love toward us, in that while we were yet sinners, Christ died for us."* God showed His great love for us, first.

It's hard to find someone who is willing to die in place of a good, or righteous person, or even a close friend, but God sent His one and only Son Jesus Christ to die in place of sinners to free them from the curse they were under according to the Law. So God demonstrated a love that surpasses justice.

And as written in Romans 5:5, *"And hope does not disappoint, because the love of God has been poured out within our hearts through the Holy Spirit who was given to us,"* God gives the Holy Spirit as a gift to all of His children that accept Jesus Christ, so they can fully understand God's love.

This is why those who are saved by faith and baptized by water and the Holy Spirit can love God not only with their minds, but truly from the center of their hearts, allowing them to abide by His commandments out of true love for Him.

God's Original Will

Originally, God created people because He desired to have true children whom He could love, and who could love Him back, out of their own free will. But if someone obeys all of

God's commandments but does not love God, how can we say he is a true child of God?

A hired hand who works for a wage cannot inherit his employer's business, but the employer's child, who is totally different from the hired hand, can inherit the business. Likewise, those who obey all of God's commandments can receive all His promised blessings, but if they don't understand God's love, they cannot be true children of God.

Therefore someone who understands God's love and abides by His commandments inherits heaven and can live in the most beautiful part of heaven as a true child of God. And living by the Father's side, he can live in glory as bright as the sun, for eternity.

God wants all people who received salvation through the blood of Jesus Christ and who love Him from the center of their hearts to live with Him in New Jerusalem, where His throne is, and share in His love for eternity. This is why Jesus said in Matthew 5:17, *"Do not think that I came to abolish the Law or the Prophets; I did not come to abolish but to fulfill."*

Evidence of How Much We Love God

Like this, only after understanding the true reason why God

gave us His commandments can we fulfill the Law, through the love we have for God. Because we have the commandments, or the laws, we can physically show 'love,' which is an abstract concept hard to see with the physical eye.

If people said, "God, I love you with all my heart, so please bless me," how can the God of justice validate their statement, if there is no standard to check them by, before blessing them? Because we have a standard, the commandments or the Law, we can see if they truly love God with all their heart. If they say with their lips that they love God, but do not keep the Sabbath day holy as God commanded us to, then we can see that they don't really love God.

So God's commandments are a standard by which we can check, or see as evidence, how much we love God.

That is why it says in 1 John 5:3, *"For this is the love of God, that we keep His commandments; and His commandments are not burdensome."*

I Love Those Who Love Me

The blessings we receive from God as a result of obeying His commandments are blessings that do not disappear or fade away.

For example, what happened to Daniel, who pleased God because he had true faith and who never compromised with the world?

Daniel was originally from the tribe of Judah, and a descendant of the family of kings. But when Southern Judah sinned against God, King Nebuchadnezzar of Babylon made his first invasion into the nation in 605 B.C. At this time, Daniel, who was very young, was taken as a captive to Babylonia.

In accordance with the King's acculturation policy, Daniel and several other young men who were also captives, were chosen to live in Nebuchadnezzar's palace and received the Chaldean schooling for three years.

During this time, Daniel asked not to be fed the daily portion of the food and wine from the king, in fear of defiling himself with foods which God forbade him to eat. As a captive, he had no right to refuse food assigned to him by the king, but Daniel wanted to do whatever he could to keep his faith pure before God.

And seeing Daniel's sincere heart, God moved the custodial officer's heart so that Daniel didn't have to eat or drink the king's food and wine.

And over time, Daniel, who thoroughly abided by God's commandments, rose to the position of prime minister of the gentile nation, Babylon. Because Daniel had unwavering faith that kept him from compromising with the world, God was pleased with him. So even though the nations changed, and kings changed, Daniel remained excellent in all his ways, and he continued to receive God's love.

Those Who Seek Me Find Me

We can still see this kind of blessing today. For anyone who has faith like Daniel that doesn't compromise with the world and abides by God's commandments with joy, we can see God blesses him with overflowing blessings.

About ten years ago, one of our elders worked for one of the top financial companies in the nation. To lure their clientele, the company held regular meetings for drinking with their clients, and golf meetings on the weekends were a must. At the time, our elder was a deacon, and after receiving this position and coming to truly understand God's love, despite the company's worldly practices, he never drank with his clients, and he never missed worshipping God on Sundays.

One day, the CEO of his company told him, "Choose between this company or your church." Being a firm person by nature, he didn't even think twice before answering, "This company is important to me, but if you ask me to choose between this company and my church, I will choose my church."

Miraculously, God moved the CEO's heart, and he put a higher level of trust in the elder, and he ended up receiving a promotion. That wasn't all. Soon after that, following a series of promotions, the elder rose to the position of CEO of a company!

So when we love God and try to abide by His commandments, God raises us to excel at whatever we do, and He blesses us in all areas of our life.

Unlike the laws made by society, God's promised words do not change with time. No matter what time period we live in, and no matter who we are, if we simply obey and live according to God's words, we can receive God's promised blessings.

The Law of Abiding with God

Therefore the Ten Commandments, or the Law which God gave to Moses, teach us the standard by which we can receive God's love and blessings.

And as it is written in Proverbs 8:17, *"I love those who love me; and those who diligently seek me will find me,"* according to how much we abide by His laws, that's how much we can receive His love and blessings.

Jesus said in John 14:21, *"He who has My commandments and keeps them is the one who loves Me; and he who loves Me will be loved by My Father, and I will love him and will disclose Myself to him."*

Do the laws of God seem heavy or forceful? But if we truly love God from the center of our hearts, we can obey them. And if we call ourselves children of God, we should naturally abide by them.

This is the way to receive God's love, the way to be with God, to meet with God, and to receive His answers to our prayers. Most importantly, His Law keeps us away from sin and moving toward the way of salvation, so what a great blessing His Law is!

Forefathers of faith like Abraham, Daniel and Joseph, because they closely abided by His Law, received blessings of being raised high above the nations. They received blessings coming in and they received blessings going out. Not only did they enjoy blessings like this in all areas of their lives, but even in heaven, they received the blessing of entering into glory as bright as the sun.

I pray in the name of our Lord Jesus Christ that you will continuously tend your ears to God's words and delight in the Law of the LORD and meditate on them day and night, and thereby abide by them completely.

"Consider how I love Your precepts;
Revive me, O LORD,
according to Your lovingkindness.
Those who love Your law have great peace,
And nothing causes them to stumble.
I hope for Your salvation, O LORD,
And do Your commandments.
Let my tongue sing of Your word,
For all Your commandments are righteousness"
(Psalm 119:159, 165, 166, 172).

The Author
Dr. Jaerock Lee

Dr. Jaerock Lee was born in Muan, Jeonnam Province, Republic of Korea, in 1943. In his twenties, he suffered from a variety of incurable diseases for seven years and awaited death with no hope for recovery. One day in the spring of 1974, however, he was led to a church by his sister, and when he knelt down to pray, the living God immediately healed him of all his diseases.

From the moment Dr. Lee met the living God through that wonderful experience, he has loved God with all his heart and sincerity, and in 1978 was called to be a servant of God. He prayed fervently so that he could clearly understand the will of God and wholly accomplish it, and obeyed all the word of God. In 1982, he founded Manmin Church in Seoul, S. Korea, and countless works of God, including miraculous healings and wonders, have been taking place at his church.

In 1986, Dr. Lee was ordained as a pastor at the Annual Assembly of Jesus' Sungkyul Church of Korea, and four years later in 1990, his sermons began to be broadcast on the Far East Broadcasting Company, the Asia Broadcast Station, and the Washington Christian Radio System to Australia, Russia, the Philippines, and many more.

Three years later in 1993, Manmin Central Church was selected as one of the "World's Top 50 Churches" by the *Christian World* magazine (US) and he received an Honorary Doctorate of Divinity from Christian Faith College, Florida, USA, and in 1996 a Ph. D. in Ministry from Kingsway Theological Seminary, Iowa, USA.

Since 1993, Dr. Lee has taken the lead in world mission through many overseas crusades in Israel, L.A., New York City, Baltimore City, and

Hawaii of the USA, Tanzania, Argentina, Uganda, Japan, Pakistan, Kenya, the Philippines, Honduras, India, Russia, Germany, Peru, and Democratic Republic of Congo, and in 2002 he was called a "worldwide pastor" by major Christian newspapers in Korea for his work in various overseas crusades.

As of November 2009, Manmin Central Church is a congregation of more than 100,000 members and has 9,000 branch churches throughout the globe including 52 domestic branch churches in major cities, and has so far commissioned more than 131 missionaries to 23 countries, including the United States, Russia, Germany, Canada, Japan, China, France, India, Kenya, and many more.

To this day, Dr. Lee has written 58 books, including bestsellers *Tasting Eternal Life before Death, My Life My Faith I & II, The Message of the Cross, The Measure of Faith, Heaven I & II,* and *Hell,* and his works have been being translated into more than 44 languages.

His Christian columns appear on *The Hankook Ilbo, The JoongAng Daily, The Dong-A Ilbo, The Munhwa Ilbo, The Seoul Shinmun, The Kyunghyang Shinmun, The Hankyoreh Shinmun, The Korea Economic Daily, The Korea Herald, The Shisa News,* and *The Christian Press.*

Dr. Lee is currently leader of many missionary organizations and associations including: Chairman, The United Holiness Church of Jesus Christ; Permanent President of the World Christianity Revival Mission Association; President, Manmin World Mission; Founder, Manmin TV; Founder & Board Chairman, Global Christian Network (GCN); Founder & Board Chairman, World Christian Doctors Network (WCDN); and Founder & Board Chairman, Manmin International Seminary (MIS).

Other powerful books by the same author

Heaven I & II

A detailed sketch of the gorgeous living environment the heavenly citizens enjoy and beautiful description of different levels of heavenly kingdoms.

The Message of the Cross

A powerful awakening message for all the people who are spiritually asleep! In this book you will find the reason Jesus is the only Savior and the true love of God.

Hell

An earnest message to all mankind from God, who wishes not even one soul to fall into the depths of hell! You will discover the never-before-revealed account of the cruel reality of the Lower Grave and hell.

Tasting Eternal Life Before Death

A testimonial memoirs of Dr. Jaerock Lee, who was born again and saved from the valley of death and has been leading an exemplary Christian life.

The Measure of Faith

What kind of a dwelling place, crown and reward are prepared for you in heaven? This book provides with wisdom and guidance for you to measure your faith and cultivate the best and most mature faith.

Awaken Israel

Why has God kept His eyes on Israel from the beginning of the world to this day? What kind of His providence has been prepared for Israel in the last days, who await the Messiah?

My Life My Faith I & II

Dr. Jaerock Lee's autobiography provides the most fragrant spiritual aroma for the readers, through his life extracted from the love of God blossomed in midst of the dark waves, cold yoke and the deepest despair.

The Power of God

A must-read that serves as an essential guide by which one can possess true faith and experience the wondrous power of God

www.urimbooks.com

www.ingramcontent.com/pod-product-compliance
Lightning Source LLC
LaVergne TN
LVHW010322070526
838199LV00065B/5630